HONEST SIGNALS

HONEST SIGNALS

How They Shape Our World

ALEX (SANDY) PENTLAND
with
TRACY HEIBECK

A Bradford Book
The MIT Press
Cambridge, Massachusetts
London, England

MIT Press books may be purchased at special quantity discounts for business or sales promotional use. For information, please email <special_sales@mitpress.mit.edu> or write to Special Sales Department, The MIT Press, 55 Hayward Street, Cambridge, MA 02142.

This book was set in Scala and Scala Sans by SNP Best-set Typesetter Ltd., Hong Kong and was printed and bound in United States of America.

Library of Congress Cataloging-in-Publication Data

Pentland, Alex (Sandy).
Honest signals : how they shape our world / Alex (Sandy) Pentland.
    p. cm.
Includes bibliographical references and index.
ISBN 978-0-262-16256-2 (hardcover : alk. paper)
1. Social perception. 2. Organizational behavior. 3. Business networks. 4. Social interaction. I. Title.
HM1041.P464   2008
302'.12—dc22

                                                                2008013832

10 9 8 7 6 5 4 3 2

CONTENTS

Preface: A God's Eye View   vii

Acknowledgments   xvii

1   HONEST SIGNALS   1

2   SOCIAL ROLES   21

3   READING PEOPLE   33

4   SURVIVAL SIGNALS   45

5   NETWORK INTELLIGENCE   57

6   SENSIBLE ORGANIZATIONS   71

7   SENSIBLE SOCIETIES   85

CONTENTS

Epilogue: Technology and Society   95
Appendix A: Social Science Background   99
Appendix B: Success   113
Appendix C: Connecting   127
Appendix D: Social Circuits   135
Appendix E: Unconscious Intelligence   145
Notes   151
References   165
Index   179

PREFACE: A GOD'S EYE VIEW

The group of rising-star business executives gathered at MIT for an important task: each executive would present a business plan to the group, and then the group would choose the best ideas to recommend to a team of venture finance experts. It was a great opportunity. The skills they each required—the ability to clearly formulate ideas, effectively communicate to a group of peers, and then persuade others to pursue those ideas—are indispensable in business as well as everyday life. These executives had each spent more than a decade building their strengths.

Not only the other group members were watching and evaluating the business plan pitches, however. A sensitive, specially designed digital device was also monitoring each presentation. This device—we'll call it a *sociometer*—wasn't recording *what* each person said in their presentation but rather *how* they said it.[1] How much variability was in the speech of the presenter? How active were they physically? How many back-and-forth gestures such as smiles and head nods occurred between the presenter and the listeners? This device was measuring another channel of communication that works without spoken language: our social sense.

At the end of the meeting, the group selected the ideas that they agreed would sell the best. At least that is what they thought. When the venture finance experts were given the plans to evaluate—this time on paper, rather than via a live presentation—there was little similarity between the two groups' judgments. Each group had a different opinion of which business plans were most likely to succeed. Why?

Our up-and-coming executives didn't pick different business plans simply because they weren't as seasoned as the venture finance experts. Remember our other observer in the room—the sociometer? As it turns out, the sociometer was able to predict which business plans the executives would choose with nearly perfect accuracy. Both the sociometer and our executives (even though they didn't know it at the time) were busy measuring the *social* content of the presentations, quite apart from the spoken, informational part.[2] And which channel of communication—social or spoken—informed more of their final decision? Yes, the social channel.

The executives thought they were evaluating the plans based on rational measures, such as: How original is this idea? How does it fit the current market? How well developed is this plan? While listening to the pitches, though, another part of their brain was registering other crucial information, such as: How much does this person believe in this idea? How confident are they when speaking? How determined are they to make this work? And the second set of information—information that the business executives didn't even know they were assessing—is what influenced their choice of business plans to the greatest degree.

When the venture finance experts saw the business plans, however, this social channel of communication was purposely removed. They saw the plans written on paper only—with no live presentation. With the social sense disconnected from the decision, the venture finance experts had to evaluate the plans based on rational measures alone. Unfortunately for them, research has shown that investments made without that "personal connection" are far more likely to fail.[3] This is why venture capital firms normally only invest in companies they can visit regularly in person, and why many investors pay more attention to the face-to-face interaction among the company's founders than they do to the business plan itself.

This study, along with many others, leads us to a surprising yet illuminating conclusion: people have a second channel of communication that revolves not around words but around *social relations*. This social channel profoundly influences major decisions in our lives *even though we are largely unaware of it*.[4] This idea lies at the heart of this book. My goal is to show you how powerful and pervasive this form of communication is in our daily lives, how it changes the way we think of ourselves and our organizations, and how you can make use of this information to better manage your life.

WHAT THIS BOOK IS ABOUT

Honest Signals comes from a new and emerging science, called *network science*, that tries to understand people in the context of their social networks rather than viewing them as isolated individuals. Historically, our understanding of human society has been limited to relatively sparse observations of individuals or small groups because we have had only simple measurement tools. Recent advances in wireless communications and digital sensors have made it now possible to observe natural, everyday human behavior at a level of detail that was previously unattainable. The result has been revolutionary measurement tools, such as the sociometer mentioned above, that provide us with a "God's eye" view of ourselves.[5]

For the first time, we can precisely map the behavior of large numbers of people as they go about their normal lives. By using cell phones and electronic badges with integrated sensors, my students and I have observed hundreds of participants for periods of up to a year. In the process we amassed hundreds of thousands of hours of detailed, quantitative data about natural, day-to-day human behavior—far more data of these kind than have ever been available before.[6]

A new measurement tool such as this often brings with it a new understanding of what you are measuring. What we have found is that many types of human behavior can be reliably predicted from biologically based *honest signaling* behaviors. These ancient primate signaling mechanisms, such as the amount of synchrony, mimicry, activity, and emphasis, form an *unconscious* channel of communication between people—a channel almost unexplored except in other apes.[7]

These social signals are not just a back channel or complement to our conscious language; they form a separate communication network that powerfully influences our behavior. In fact, these honest signals provide a quite effective window into our intentions, goals, and values. By examining this ancient channel of communication, for instance—paying no attention to words or even who the people are—we can accurately *predict* outcomes of dating situations, job interviews, and even salary negotiations.[8]

We have shown that people's behavior is much more a function of their social network than anyone has previously imagined. Humans are truly social animals, where individuals are best likened to musicians in a jazz quartet, forming a web of unconscious reactions tuned to exactly complement the others in the group. What the sociometer data demonstrate is that this immersion of self in the surrounding social network is the *typical* human condition, rather than being isolated examples found in exceptional circumstances.

Why does this ancient communication channel exist? What does it do? Data from biology show that honest signals evolved to co-ordinate behavior between competing groups of individuals.[9] For instance, honest signals form a communication channel that helps to create family groups and hunting teams. The *social circuits* formed by the back-and-forth pattern of signaling between people shapes much of our behavior, as our ancient reflexes for unconscious, social coordination work to fuse us together into a co-ordinated (but often contentious) whole.

In a family, a work group, or even an entire organization, the pattern of signaling within the social network strongly influences the behavior of both the individuals and the group as a whole.[10] Healthy signaling patterns result in good decision making, while bad patterns result in disaster. The social circuitry of a work group, for instance, can insulate the group from problems like groupthink and polarization. Even for large networks of humans, such as companies or entire societies, the pattern of social circuitry influences the "intelligence" of the network.

By paying careful attention to the pattern of signaling within a social network, we can harvest tacit knowledge that is spread across all of the individual members of the network. This *network intelligence* approach to capturing the "wisdom of the crowd" produces surprisingly good results and is often many times better than traditional decision-making methods. I will examine this idea of network intelligence carefully, and see how to harness it to improve group decision making.

PLAN FOR THE BOOK

The goal of this book is to show how these honest signals influence critical activities such as negotiation, group decision making, and project management, and to demonstrate how powerful and pervasive this form of communication is in our lives. Throughout, I will present new science backing many intuitive ideas that were previously thought to be just folk wisdom. By refining these intuitions with scientific measurements and explanatory mechanisms, readers will discover a new and powerful way to understand and manage human groups, corporations, and even entire societies.

The first order of business will be to explain how social circuits work, and how to be more aware of them. Drawing from research into animal behavior, we find that animals communicate by signals, with honest signals being of particular interest. Honest signals are behaviors that are so expensive or so directly connected to the underlying biology that they become reliable indicators that others use to guide their own behavior. People possess these same signals in addition to conscious language. They are so essential for people, in fact, that infants rely on these signals in order to learn language. Even from the beginning, our two channels of communication— social and linguistic—are intertwined.

A startling finding is that the social circuits formed by back-and-forth signaling between people is a major factor in even the most important decisions in our lives. Using the sociometer mentioned earlier, we will see that in many situations—including negotiation, sales, dating, and teamwork—people's signaling can accurately predict how they are going to act and what the eventual outcome will be.

Some people are experts at reading these social signals and using them to influence others, even though most are unaware of how they do it. We can begin to understand how they manage this by examining how social signaling can be used to control behavior. By looking at characteristic types of social tasks—such as pitching a new idea, networking, and closing a deal—we find that particular kinds of signals are associated with success. We can also see how to change our personal style to become more effective.

The same social circuits that form between pairs of people are also active in groups. By examining the signaling of groups making various types of decisions, I will show how signaling works to shape the behavior of human social groups. By comparing the performance of groups with different patterns of signaling, I will demonstrate how some patterns of signaling improve the decision-making capacity of groups and aid the flow of information within our social networks.

We will see that the ability to "read" the social signaling within one's social network provides a mechanism for group decision making that is different than the standard theory of rational decision making. Instead of logic or argument, this is a marketlike mechanism that aggregates information and minimizes risk to achieve maximum expected results. The behavior of groups, organizations, and entire cultures can be analyzed in terms of this new network intelligence theory of rational decision making. By looking at examples of real organizations, we will gain surprising insights and practical methods for managing and governing ourselves.

Finally, the book will look to the future, where digital tools like the sociometer may become common in everyday life. The futuristic capability to read the social side of life can revolutionize how we live as well as how we manage ourselves. It can let us screen for depression, x-ray an organization's health, or allow a company to "tune" itself to maximize employee happiness. It could even be forged into a new sort of nervous system that could span all of humanity. At the same time, these new technologies present unprecedented threats to privacy and social liberty, and so must be carefully used and controlled. The debate about how to harness this new human nervous system is one of the most important going on today.

READING HONEST SIGNALS

Honest Signals is written to be accessible to a broad audience, not just managers and academics, but also anyone curious about how new science might change their lives. As a consequence, experimental details, statistical analysis, and examination of the academic literature have been confined to the appendixes of the book.

Don't assume, however, that these appendixes are purely academic, because they also provide detail useful for applying this information in everyday life. The appendixes are:

- *Social science background* The social science background, the sociometer, and an explanation of the experimental and analysis methods
- *Succeeding* Assessing interest, pitching business plans, selling, negotiation, and deception
- *Connecting* Getting hired, getting a date, and social networking
- *Social circuits* Understanding identity, work groups, friends, and your position in the network
- *Unconscious intelligence* A new understanding about how our minds work gives hope that we can act with greater intelligence

In addition to the summary descriptions in the appendixes, there are the original papers, theses, experimental data, and computer codes available at <http://hd.media.mit.edu>.

Because of the large number of coauthors and papers summarized in this book, it proved difficult to name each coauthor and paper in the main text and still maintain an ease of readability. Consequently my research group will just be referred to as "we," but will be accompanied by a specific citation. Members of my research group include current and former graduate students: Sumit Basu, Ron Caneel, David Chilongo, Tanzeem Choudhury, Brian Clarkson, Wen Dong, Nathan Eagle, Jon Gips, Taemie Kim, Anmol Madan, Akshay Mohan, Daniel Olguin, Will Stoltzman, Mike Sung, and Ben Waber as well as postdoctoral, adjunct, and visiting researchers Koji Ara, Joost Bonsen, and M. C. Martin.

ACKNOWLEDGMENTS

I am deeply indebted to my current and former graduate students, postdoctoral, adjunct, and visiting researchers. I would also like to thank my research collaborators for their support and help in framing the ideas in this book, especially Jared Curhan, David Lazer, Carl Marci, Deb Roy, and Dr. Yano. Finally, I would like to thank Tracy Heibeck for her hard work at brainstorming examples, editing the manuscript, writing some of the stories introducing the chapters, and putting up with me while I worked to pull years of research into a coherent narrative. Like Ginger Rogers, she danced every step of writing this book, although it was not usually backward.

HONEST SIGNALS

HONEST SIGNALS

It is just past dinner as you enter the local pub and find it filled with separate clusters of twenty-something men and twenty-something women. Everyone appears both a little nervous and a little excited—welcome to the world of speed dating. During the next hour, each man and woman will spend five minutes chatting with ten members of the opposite sex. At the end of every encounter, each person *secretly* writes down whether or not they want to exchange phone numbers. If *both* say yes, then the organizers will pass on the numbers at the end of the night.

Now, the common assumption is that men are fairly indiscriminate in situations such as this—they will say yes to almost any woman—whereas women are far more selective. But tonight the common assumption about men was wrong. As it turned out, men generally said yes to exchanging phone numbers only when the women also said yes.[1] Remember, the rules of speed dating require that this information is kept secret and is seen only by the organizers at the end of the evening. So how did these men know, in just five minutes, when the women they were talking with would say yes? Was it a kind of mysterious chemistry? Was there some sort of secret signal that tipped them off?

Perhaps biology, rather than chemistry, holds part of the answer. Consider the concept of an honest signal. These are signals, as noted earlier, that are either so costly to make or so difficult to suppress that they are reliable in signaling intention.[2] A classic example is the squawking made by hungry baby birds. When their parent returns to the nest with some food, the fledglings immediately launch into a chorus of loud cries. On the one hand, the cries make the fledglings more vulnerable to nearby predators. On the other hand, the benefit of signaling hunger to a parent outweighs the increased risk from hawks and other enemies.

The potential costs associated with honest signals aren't restricted to predators. Some animals, such as the male peacock with its extravagant feathers, assume a high metabolic cost for their honest signals. Other large expenditures could be in energy, as typified by many animals' mating displays. Consider the exhausting strategies of the male orangutan: he will shake branches, topple over dead trees, and make calls loud enough to be heard for several miles. For female orangutans, bigger seems to be better; the louder the male's calls, the more alluring they are for the female.

These trustworthy signals tend to evolve by natural selection whenever the fitness of a species requires bringing together individuals in the midst of broad competition. The so-called battle of the sexes is an example, and obviously the fitness of the species depends on creating mating pairs. All of which brings us back to our speed-dating experiment. Our twenty-something women were not in the trees shaking branches but were still sending signals of some kind. The honest signals of humans are not quite so loud and obvious, yet the trained eye—or sociometer—can detect them easily. So could our twenty-something men. What did they see?

Imagine that you are watching two women from across the room as they each converse with their speed dates. From your vantage point, you can't hear what they are saying but you can see all their movements. One woman seems to be rather talkative, gesturing and moving around as she speaks. You notice that she seems to nod her head quite a bit, often in concert with the man at her table. The other woman, however, does not seem to be doing any of these things. She is rather still, appears to say just a few words, and there is almost no back-and-forth gesturing between her and her date. Based on these descriptions, who is having the better time with her date? Who is going to say yes to exchanging phone numbers? Chances are, you are as good at figuring this out as the men in the speed-dating experiment were.

WHAT ARE HONEST HUMAN SIGNALS?

What are the types of honest signals that humans use? We are familiar with many types of human signals; smiles, frowns, fast cars, and fancy clothes are all signals of who we are (or who we want to be). In fact, this sort of signaling is probably the basis of fashion and "current culture."[3] We are conscious of these types of displays and often carefully plan to incorporate them into our communications. And therein lies the problem: because these signals are so frequently planned, we cannot rely on them being honest signals. We need to look for signals that are processed *unconsciously*, or that are otherwise uncontrollable, before we can count them as honest.

If we watch the give-and-take of conversational turn taking and gesturing, and carefully measure the timing, energy, and variability of the interaction, we can find several examples of honest signals. Four that we will concentrate on here are:

- *Influence*   The amount of influence each person has on another in a social interaction. Influence is measured by the extent to which one person causes the other person's pattern of speaking to match their own pattern.
- *Mimicry*   The reflexive copying of one person by another during a conversation, resulting in an unconscious back-and-forth trading of smiles, interjections, and head nodding during a conversation.
- *Activity*   Increased activity levels normally indicate interest and excitement, as seen in the connection between the activity level and excitement in children, or when male orangutans shake branches in order to impress potential mates.
- *Consistency*   When there are many different thoughts or emotions going on in your mind at the same time, your speech and even your movements become jerky, unevenly accented and paced. The consistency of emphasis and timing is a signal of mental focus, while greater variability may signal an openness to influence from others.

Each of these signals has its roots in our brain structure and biology. This may be why they are such reliable signals of our behavioral tendencies. Our influence measure, for instance, provides an assessment of our brains' attention and orienting systems. These subcortical structures (centered around the tectum, which is also known as the superior colliculus depending on the species) integrate sensory information and produce orienting responses.[4] When your eyes move to a person entering a room or your head turns toward a sudden noise, your behavior is being guided by these ancient brain structures. By measuring the accuracy and consistency of response between people, our influence measure provides an assessment of the functioning of their attentional mechanisms.

In contrast, mimicry is thought to be due to cortical mirror neurons, a distributed brain structure that seems to be unique to primates and is especially prominent in humans.[5] Mirror neurons react to other people's actions and provide a direct feedback channel between people. Newborns for instance, can mimic their parents' facial movements despite their general lack of coordination. Mirror neurons situated in the part of the brain's motor cortex that controls the face may be key to this surprising capability.

Our activity level is related to the state of our autonomic nervous system, an extremely old neural structure. Whenever we need to react more vigorously—such as in fight-or-flight situations or when sexually aroused—this system supplies a dose of "nervous energy" that manifests itself in our behavior. On the other hand, we act listless and low energy when our autonomic nervous system is blunted, as in depression.[6] The relationship between autonomic nervous system function and activity level is tight enough that we have been able to use it in clinical trials to accurately estimate the severity of depression, and even predict treatment response.[7]

And finally, consistency seems to be a measure of the integration within our brains' action sequence control system, which begins with cortical motor signals that propagate through the cerebellum and basal ganglia.[8] Professional dancers or athletes, for example, exhibit a smoothness and consistency of action that comes from an enormous amount of practice. The effect of all their practice is to "burn" the action sequences into the neural connections in the cerebellum and basal ganglia. The same seems to be true of dialogue segments; their smoothness and consistency is an indication of how well we have integrated them into our behavioral repertoire.

These four signals are not the only honest signals that humans exhibit. For instance, Robert Provine has shown that laughter is an ancient signal similar to mimicry: when one person laughs, our reflex to copy the laughter is so automatic that often it is hard to not laugh, even when it is inappropriate. Apes also laugh, almost always when engaged in hard play.[9] Human laughter seems to have evolved from this physical context to fill the more general but still playlike function of increasing bonding and reducing tension between people. My focus in this book, however, will be on honest signals that are constantly present in all interactions, even in the most serious, and so I have chosen to concentrate on just these four types of honest signals.

INFLUENCE

A classic example of influence in conversation is the experience of being grilled by a superior. Put yourself in the shoes of a school-age child caught by a teacher trying to sneak into school late. Imagine what might happen next. The teacher's questions come fast and furious, demanding to know where you were, why you were late, and don't you know this is against the rules, and on and on until you think it might never end. The feeling you have is similar to being pinned to the floor and beaten by the barrage of questions, even though no one was touching you.

The sensation of being pinned by the questions comes from verbal pushing. In our cranky teacher situation, the teacher was cutting you off a few milliseconds before you got to "pauses" in your speaking, well before you were done with your thought. Verbal cues that demand an immediate response, phrases like "you know you are late, right?" are also part of the verbal pushing. By skillfully using these strategies to influence how and when you responded, the teacher was controlling the pattern of conversation.

What is striking about these patterns of conversation is that the differences caused by various types of influence are so exact as to be measured in milliseconds.[10] This fine-grain perceptual task is impossible to do through conscious processing; it instead demands the engagement of our brains' ancient attention and orienting systems. As a consequence, these tiny time differences in the pattern of interaction become available to our conscious minds only indirectly as the intuition that the other person is insistent, paying attention, or is interested.

Influence serves many important purposes for people. As in the student-teacher example above, influence is famously an indicator of dominance.[11] In studies of negotiation, a consistent finding is that the person who most consistently holds the floor has a sizable advantage. But influence applies to more than the pattern of turn taking in a conversation. Analyses of debates among candidates for the U.S. presidency, for instance, have found that the influence on speaking pitch (the fundamental tone of one's voice) predicts who will win the election.[12] The explanation is that the candidate who sets the tone of the debate is seen as the most dominant, and that voters react to this signal of dominance.

Even as infants we are sensitive to conversational influence, using it as a guide for learning language. We are all familiar with the "baby language" or "motherese" used by adults—a singsong rhythm full of goo-goos and dah-dahs.[13] But along with the practice of these simple building-block sounds comes the experience for infants in how to take turns in a conversation as well as instruction in which activities and objects the adult thinks are critical for the baby to pay attention to.[14] Without the scaffolding provided by conversational influence, the infant will remain confused about how sounds map to ideas and may struggle unsuccessfully to learn to speak.

The strength of influence between a mother and her infant child is considered so essential that doctors use it to detect problems in language development when the infant is as young as four months.[15] One important case where language development is inhibited occurs when the mother is depressed and fails to energetically engage the infant in wordplay. The babies of these depressed mothers quickly discover that the mother isn't providing the social scaffolding that guides learning and begin paying more attention to other adults in their environment.[16]

All of this influence is costly, however. It takes enormous mental resources to package up our conscious thoughts, translate them into spoken words and gestures, and then insert them into an ongoing conversation at exactly the appropriate time. Nor is the cost only in terms of the mental and physical energy expended. The sort of spectacular social sensitivity and fine-tuned responsiveness needed to engage in conversation requires continual attention and focus.

Everyone has had the experience of accidentally bumping into obstacles when deeply engaged in a conversation. This sort of "tunnel attention" is expensive in biological terms, because the perfect time for a predator to sneak up on a human is when they are engrossed in conversation. As a result of its cost, the strength of influence in a conversation serves as an honest signal of attention. You can't maintain the intricate dance of conversational turn taking if you aren't paying attention.

OUR SOCIOMETER DATA

Our experiments show that people seem to use this honest signal to assess the attitudes and interest levels of others. For instance, when we looked at the pattern of influence during forty-six different salary negotiations, we found that the strength of influence was tightly correlated with the sense people had of how hard the other person was trying.[7] If the negotiation was one-sided, rather like the grilling of a student by a teacher, then the person controlling the conversational pattern would be perceived as trying hard, whereas the person being controlled would be perceived as giving up. If both parties were influencing the pattern of conversation equally, so that they were practically talking over each other and there were no gaps in the back-and-forth, then both parties would be perceived as trying hard to come out on top in the negotiation.

Given the significance of this signal of interest and attention in everything from salary negotiations to the clinical diagnosis of language learning problems, it is startling how unaware people are of their pattern of influence, and how it varies from situation to situation. We seem to know when people are interested, but we can't explain how we know. Just as we are unaware of our visual blind spot or missing harmonics in music, these low-level signals of social structure seem to be handled by our brains' ancient attention systems, and so are mostly invisible to our conscious mind. Influence appears to be a genuine, honest signal of attention.

MIMICRY

Mimicry, such as the reflexive copying of smiles, interjections, and head nodding during a conversation, is a special type of influence. It is actually rather amusing to watch: when two people are deeply engaged in conversation and on the same wavelength (in contrast to being in a heated debate), they will copy each other. If one person crosses their arms or sits back in their chair, then a few seconds later the other person will do the same thing. If one person smiles or starts nodding their head, then so will the other.[18]

People tend to mimic each other automatically and unconsciously—a behavior that is believed to be due to our brains' generous endowment of mirror neurons.[19] But despite being unconscious, this mimicking behavior has an important effect on the participants: it increases how much the conversational partners will say that they like and trust each other. Negotiations where the participants are unconsciously mimicking each other therefore tend to be smoother and more successful, all other factors being equal.[20] Not surprisingly, more empathetic people are more likely to mimic their conversational partners; as a consequence, mimicry is often described an unconscious signal of empathy.

Mimicry can play a key role in sales as well. For instance, when Jeremy Bailenson and Nick Yee at Stanford University used computer-animated figures to give students a three-minute pitch to encourage them to carry the university identification card whenever they are on campus, they tried it both with and without mimicry.[21] Some of the students just saw a cartoonlike video trying to convince them to carry the identification card. For other students, however, the animated figure *moved exactly as they did*, but with a delay of four seconds. If a student tilted their head thoughtfully and looked up at a fifteen-degree angle, say, then the animated figure would repeat the gesture four seconds later.

Despite the rather obvious nature of the copycat animation, only eight of the sixty-nine subjects detected the mimicry (and those mostly because they made a strange movement and then saw the agent making the same unusual motion). The remaining students liked the mimicking agent more than the recorded agent, and rated the former as being friendlier as well as more interesting, honest, and persuasive. They also paid better attention to the copycat presenter and found the mimicker to be more persuasive. In the final analysis, just adding mimicry made the sales pitch *20 percent* more effective.

OUR SOCIOMETER DATA

Using the sociometer we have been able to measure the same effects in the real world, observing the mimicry that occurs during typical face-to-face interactions. In one experiment, for example, Jared Curhan and I looked at practice salary negotiations between midlevel executives that are just transferring into a new company and their new boss.[22] We used the sociometer to measure the honest signals from both participants during the first few minutes of the negotiation, when people were just getting to know each other, and laying out their initial proposal for salary and benefits.

What we found was that the signaling of the new employee was different from that of the boss, and while several of the honest signals predicted the final salary package, our computerized measure of the amount of mimicry was one of the most important signals. For the new employee, the measured amount of mimicry alone accounted for almost *one-third* of the variation in the final salary.

Moreover, the amount of mimicry was strongly correlated with the feelings both participants had about the negotiation. Negotiations with a lot of mimicry left both the boss and the new employee with a strong feeling that everyone had cooperated to avoid getting stuck in sharp disagreements. Such a feeling of cooperation is obviously critical for starting off their new relationship on a good footing.

In both salary negotiations and sales, we have seen that mimicry functions as an honest and effective signal of the trust as well as empathy required for successful negotiations and financial transactions. What is particularly impressive is the effectiveness of this honest signal: unconscious, automatic mimicry improved financial results by *20 to 30 percent*. The impact of mimicry on these financial interactions dwarfs almost every other factor that has ever been studied.

ACTIVITY LEVEL

The amount of energy devoted to maintaining the social fabric is also a signal that hovers at the edge of our consciousness. It takes a considerable amount of energy to maintain the millisecond-accurate back-and-forth of a conversation. As a result, energy expenditure is an honest signal of the value that one attaches to a social interaction. Increased activity levels thus normally indicate interest and excitement.

In children, the connection between activity level and excitement is particularly transparent. Who is not familiar with kids almost bouncing off the walls in anticipation of a birthday party or other special event? When excited, kids talk faster and louder, fidget more, and run around at the slightest provocation. What is happening is a general arousal within their autonomic nervous system, resulting in a higher level of motor activity.[23]

Adults show the same physiological effects, and although we have been trained to control ourselves better than kids, excited adults still fidget more, talk more, and talk more quickly. The connection between an increased activity level and interest is especially clear when talking with other people. When we are engaged in conversation, our minds are occupied with the words, facts, and other conscious aspects of the discussion. As such, it is hard to pay attention to the arousal level of our autonomic nervous system, and even harder to accurately control its effects. The result is that our activity level, even when suppressed and visible only as fidgets and nervousness, is an honest signal of interest.

OUR SOCIOMETER DATA

When we use the sociometer to look at real-world interactions like dating and social networking, we find that activity level is an honest signal of interest and excitement. In the speed-dating event described above, the woman's activity level was the most important predictor of whether or not she was going to share her phone number.[24]

More generally, when we looked at people engaged in discussions about news topics, we found that their activity level was one signal of how interesting they found the conversation. It is, in fact, quite a familiar effect: when we speak about having an "animated discussion," we mean that the participants were interested and excited about the topic being discussed.[25]

The same applies to social interactions such as making friends or social networking. When two people are exploring the possibility of a closer relationship, one sign of their interest in each other is their rising activity level. For instance, when we used the sociometer to monitor a group of more than one hundred people attending a conference at our laboratory, we found that activity level was one of the key signals of mutual interest and was predictive of trading contact information.[26] Whenever we detected two people gesturing and talking particularly energetically, the odds were very good that they would trade contact information within the next two minutes. Regardless of who they were or where they were from, their activity level accurately predicted the trading of contact information. Thus, activity level serves as an honest signal of interest.

CONSISTENCY

Emphasis, which is the energy spent in modulating speech production, is often mentioned as a signal of how strongly the speaker is motivated. Strong emotions or crucial points in a conversation tend to be emphasized by greater volume or accent. Just as with activity level, however, adults spend a great deal of effort learning to hide this signal. Who hasn't been told, at least as a child, to "speak calmly and clearly" when you got especially excited?

There are also many other reasons why a speaker might increase or decrease their emphasis.[27] Speaking in the midst of a noisy crowd, for example, requires not only volume but greater emphasis as well. Fortunately, our vocal tract automatically increases the amount of emphasis with increasing volume. At the other end of the spectrum, a whispered conversation has less volume but often increased emphasis in order to maintain intelligibility. As a consequence of the necessity to adapt to different speaking environments, the absolute amount of volume or emphasis a speaker uses is an unreliable signal of motivation, and hence not a good candidate for an honest signal.

But there is another way to understand this basic signal. If we accept that strong emotions or significant points in a conversation tend to be emphasized by greater volume or accent, then a speaker with a single, consistent motivation throughout a conversation will tend to have a more uniform emphasis. Similarly, when a speaker has competing motivations of differing strength, they will tend to speak or move with variable emphasis.

We can understand this variability as a signal of conflict within our brains' action sequence system. When there are several conflicting "commands" coming down from our higher brain centers, each requiring our body to take different sorts of actions, this interferes with our ability to act in a smooth, consistent manner. This interference effect is regularly used to measure our cognitive load—roughly, how many things you are thinking about at the same time; when there are lots of different things going on in your head simultaneously, your speech and movements become jerky and unevenly paced.[28] The relative consistency or variability of this basic signal conveys different messages for people, as we will soon see.

Imagine, for instance, that you are in the middle of a salary negotiation and the other person has just thrown you off balance by proposing something completely unexpected. Somehow you have to quickly figure out what to do without letting on that this has left you flailing about for the right response. Here's what is likely to happen next with your behavior: your speaking pace, emphasis, and even hand and body movements become uneven as your mental resources strive to work on the new problem and at the same time carry on the conversation as if nothing happened. It is this variability in emphasis and rhythm that people are really unable to control. Consequently, the consistency of one's emphasis and timing is an honest signal of a focused and smoothly functioning mind.

OUR SOCIOMETER DATA

When we looked at salary negotiations with the sociometer, we found these same patterns.[29] That is, the more consistent people were in their pattern of emphasis, the better they did in the salary negotiation. This was true for both the boss and the new employee—showing variability weakens your negotiation stance. We found the same to be true for business executives pitching business plans. The more consistent they were in emphasis and rhythm while giving their pitch, the more convincing they were to others. That was not the only benefit; people with greater consistency were also perceived as having better ideas and a better presentation style.[30]

Consistent emphasis, however, is not always a good thing. It indicates focus and determination, but that is the opposite of what you want to signal when you are in the role of the listener and helper. In these situations, you want to be open to the concerns and ideas of others. In handling sales inquiries from customers where the potential customers are already interested enough to call an agent, for example, a soft sell attitude of helpful listening is better than a hard sell pitch. In fact, when we studied sales inquiries to a major retail chain, we found that variability in emphasis together with the amount of listening time predicted a successful sales call with extremely high accuracy.[31]

And so variability in emphasis and pace appears to be an honest signal that you are open to the contributions of others, perhaps because it is the opposite of the consistent emphasis that signals that you have made up your mind. Even at a fine level of interaction, variability seems to signal an *openness* to input from other people. Indeed, when we looked at thousands of hours of recorded conversations, we found that the simple signal of variable emphasis, together with the length of time you had already spoken, accurately predicted places where other people would jump into the conversation.[32]

In summary, consistency of emphasis and timing in conversation is an indication of the amount of integration between higher brain centers and our action sequence control system. Consistency is therefore an honest signal of mental focus and determination, while variability indicates competing mental processes and is a signal that others may be able to influence your thinking.

NEXT STEPS

Honest signals are behaviors that are sufficiently expensive to fake that they can form the basis for a reliable channel of communication.

These signals evolve in environments where fitness depends on bringing together individuals in the presence of general competition; competition for a mate is perhaps the most classic situation in which honest signals have been described.

Conversations between people are a likely place to find honest signals. This is because many, if not most, conversations have an element of competition, and because conversation is biologically expensive. Social competition is nearly universal; we are always striving to put on a good face and show that we are part of the team. And anyone who has gone through a series of job interviews or been part of a negotiation can testify that continued concentration and interaction is exhausting. As a consequence, conversations are exactly the sort of place where we would expect to find honest signals.

We have focused on four honest signals—influence, mimicry, activity, and consistency—and found that as expected of such signals, they are strongly predictive of future behavior. We know that these behaviors function as signals because they unconsciously change other people's impressions of your attention, trust, interest, and focus. Moreover, we know that they are honest signals because they reliably predict people's future actions across a wide range of circumstances.[33]

These signals seem to be an ancient legacy of human evolution. They are a reading of basic brain functions, such as the arousal of the autonomic nervous system, the engagement of the attention and orienting brain centers, and the integration of the action sequencing system as well as the function of the more recently evolved mirror neuron system. Our signals are thus similar to those of our ape cousins, and may even be similar to the signaling found in a much broader animal community.[34] Examples such as the horse named Clever Hans being able to "read" his owner or the myriad stories about dogs being able to read their human masters seem to show that we can communicate interest, attention, and perhaps determination across species.

The antiquity of honest signals is also suggested by another property: honest signals are easy to read even in noisy or poorly lit environments. People (and also sociometers) can easily read these signals in bars, at mixers, at night, on the subway, or out of the corner of the eye. In contrast, the ability to understand words or read facial expressions depends on a precise, fine-grained analysis of sound and sight, which is difficult to do at a distance, or in a noisy or poorly illuminated environment. Our set of honest signals is much better suited to communication in forests or around camp-fires than are the fine nuances of language and affect.

The next chapter will explore how these honest signals function in everyday life. We will find that they can be combined to com-municate the social role of the speaker—leading, teaming, listen-ing, and exploring—and that this role behavior is extremely predictive of the interaction outcome.

SOCIAL ROLES

Tom was transferring into another branch of the company and he needed to finalize his compensation package. It would also be the first time he would meet his new boss, so the stakes were high. Not only did he want to make a good impression and show that he was a team member but he also wanted to get a good deal.

As soon as the negotiation started, Tom knew he might be in trouble. The boss seemed to control the conversation from the outset and appeared determined to set the terms of the pay package. Tom felt pushed into a corner. So Tom mentally gathered his strength and put on his most confident face, while at the same time making it clear that he was the sort of person who would be a real team player.

The boss could tell that Tom was sure of what he wanted and what he deserved in terms of a pay package. He could also tell that

Tom would fit in and make the department stronger. So he worked with Tom, and together they assembled a pay package that was good for both the company and Tom.

Why did Tom feel pushed into a corner, and how did he get out? How did Tom and his new boss know about the other's determination? Or how supportive the other would be? How did they know how interested the other was in one feature of the pay package versus another? As we observed with the business plan pitches, the sociometer shows that this is a story of signaling and response, rather than arguments and reasons.[1]

SIGNALING SOCIAL ROLE

When we look across all of our experiments, we see that people in real-life situations employ *combinations* of honest signals rather than using them individually. These combinations cluster in characteristic ways to signal the social role that the person has adopted—the attitudes, intentions, and goals that characterize typical types of relationships between people.[2] While people can assume many social roles, I will focus on a core group of four social roles: exploring, listening, teaming, and leading.

To illustrate how honest signals communicate social roles, I will start with the central interpretation of each of our honest signals. Let's say that influence signals attention, mimicry signals empathic understanding, activity level signals interest, and consistent emphasis signals mental focus and determination (and hence inconsistent or variable emphasis signals a possible openness to influence). Obviously this simplification ignores context effects and other important variables, but this will serve to start.

The social role of exploring, such as when you want to explore the possibility of having a deeper relationship with someone, can be communicated by displaying a combination of honest signals of interest and an openness to influence. That is, you would adopt a high activity level along with variable emphasis and rhythm.

For the social role of active listening, you would display a combination of attentive interest and an openness to new ideas. You would therefore have variable emphasis along with an activity level that is suppressed (e.g., fidgeting and similar "nervous" behaviors).

The teaming role requires the display of a combination of attention, empathic understanding, and focused thought and purpose. Thus, you would exhibit high influence, ample mimicry, and consistent emphasis and rhythm.

And finally, when adopting the role of leading you would display a combination of attention, interest, and great focus in thought and purpose. Your behavior would thus include high levels of influence, high activity levels, and a consistency of emphasis and rhythm.

Surprisingly, just these four social roles, which were defined by observing how people combine honest signals in common situations, can be used to accurately predict outcomes in many of our most important interactions. In sales, negotiation, dating, hiring, and many other situations, the signaling associated with these social roles accurately predicts who will succeed, and who will not. To better understand how social roles function, let's examine each social role in more detail, and walk through how the honest signals associated with each role determine how the person-to-person interaction will play itself out.

EXPLORING

The exploring role, where people are signaling their interest in further and deeper interaction, is characterized by a high activity level (interest) along with variable emphasis and rhythm (an openness to influence), as noted above. People tend to be conscious of only extreme examples of this exploring behavior; gross violations of social norms tend to get our attention. Perceiving the subtle variations in behavior that mark intermediate states of interest requires paying close attention to the nuances of unconscious behavior. This is a difficult task at best, and almost impossible to do while participating in the conversation yourself. Consideration of this fact is one reason that skilled negotiators bring along an assistant; the assistant can concentrate on the social signaling, while the negotiator focuses on the content of the discussion.

As you might expect, the exploring display is a powerful predictor in some situations. When we used the sociometer to examine how people mixed at events like trade shows, we found that when two people were standing together and displaying exploring signals—a high activity level and highly variable emphasis—the odds were extremely high that they would trade contact information within the next two minutes.[3] The predictive power of this exploring display held true for people from North America, Asia, and Europe, men and women, and twenty-somethings and sixty-somethings.

Similarly, when we gave out sociometers at a speed-dating event, we again found the exploring display playing a central role. When the woman had a high activity level and strongly variable emphasis—again, the signaling components of the exploring display—this accurately predicted *both* parties' decision about whether or not to trade phone numbers.[4] As we might have guessed, the man's signaling wasn't significantly predictive of trading numbers. We know that the men picked up the women's exploring displays because, as mentioned previously, men only offered to trade phone numbers when the women had also decided to do so. Thus, despite the fact that the women's decisions were kept secret by the organizers of the speed-dating event until the end of the evening, the women's social signaling had already delivered their decisions loud and clear.

ACTIVE LISTENING

The active listening role is characterized by a display that combines suppressed interest or excitement, along with an openness to influence, achieved by signaling behavior that includes a suppressed level of activity and variable emphasis. This type of active listening display is seen in a variety of situations. For instance, when we used the sociometer to examine people's behavior at events like a trade show, we found that when a person displayed active listening signals when standing in front of a display, the odds were high that they would ask for additional information within the next two minutes.[5] As a result, monitoring people's active listening displays could be a useful tool for designing learning and entertainment environments.

Active listening is also critical on the job. For example, when we looked at customer interactions with a high-quality retailer, we found that the strength of the active listening signaling was an extremely accurate predictor of the success of the interaction.[6] It is interesting that the soft sell social signals that were most successful in this case are the opposite of the hard sell ones that worked when pitching a business plan, suggesting that different signaling is required at different stages of the sales process.

In a different situation, we found the same type of active listening display when we looked at semipro poker games. We found that players who behaved in this manner were likely to be either bluffing or engaged in some other high-risk play.[7] In fact, this was a reliable enough predictor of the game play that we could have made a great deal of money just by watching for the behavior and then aggressively raising the bet.

Why were these highly practiced players giving away their state of play? In part, this is just the nature of an honest signal: it is an unconscious window into our attitudes, intentions, and goals. But in this case it is likely that the behavior we observed is also due to an active, conscious strategy to hide excitement and stress. The players were trying to "act normally," but because people can't accurately judge their normal activity level, they overdid it.

TEAMING

The teaming role is characterized by the display of a combination of attention, empathic understanding, and focused thought and purpose. Therefore, this style of behavior includes high influence, ample mimicry, and consistent emphasis and rhythm.

This sort of display is familiar from interactions with (good) contractors, consultants, and medical workers. What they want to achieve during their interaction with you is approval to begin working on your problem. To accomplish this, they need to communicate to you that they are listening to your problems, are on your side and here to help, and know what they are doing. The competent and compassionate nurse, the knowledgeable and honest electrician, or the experienced and professional accountant is each an expert at conveying solidarity and joining the client in a team effort.

Displays of solidarity and teaming are, of course, critical in business interactions. In the salary negotiation example, for instance, the teaming behavior style was the required antidote to a determined boss.[8] Analogous to the bosses' displays of determination, the new employees' displays of solidarity and teaming at the start of the negotiation were a strong predictor of the final negotiated salary. Even before getting to the stage of negotiating a salary, we found that the strength of the teaming display at the start of a job interview was a powerful predictor of hiring decisions.[9]

LEADING

The leading role includes signals that convey a combination of interest, attention, and great focus in thought and purpose. Consequently, the leading display includes high activity levels, high levels of influence, and a consistency of emphasis and rhythm.

The leading role is similar to the teaming one, but with higher levels of activity and lower levels of empathetic mimicry. In our sociometer data, leading is a natural extension of teaming. It is what happens when you are focused on an interaction, know what you want, and think you can push the others to give it to you. As with the other signaling styles, we can become consciously aware of this sort of behavior when confronted with extreme cases—for example, the person who is in your face and won't stop—probably because they are such radical violations of social norms. The difficulty is in perceiving the subtle variations in behavior that mark intermediate levels of determination.

We found a clear example of why it pays to attend to social signals when we looked at salary negotiations between a new employee and their future boss. What we discovered was that the strength of the bosses' leading signaling at the start of the negotiation was a very good predictor of the final negotiated salary; in fact, it was a better predictor of the negotiated salary than any other factor.[10]

In other words, the bosses who took control of the negotiation and consistently emphasized their position right from the beginning negotiated the best deals for their company. That isn't the whole story, of course. Unless the boss also displayed some level of teaming and supportiveness for the new employee, it is likely that their relationship would get off to a rocky start.

Similarly, when we looked at people pitching business plans, we found that the strength of the leading signals accurately predicted how well a business plan was rated.[11] So powerful were the effects of the social signaling that raters completely confused what the content of the plan was with how it was pitched to them. Indeed, the *automatic* ratings generated by the sociometer were as good as the typical businessperson's ability to predict how the plan would be rated.

SIGNALS?

Could the predictability we see still just be a side effect of something else rather than an unconscious reaction to the social context? That is, could the signals we measure with the sociometer somehow be due to the particular way we structure and accent words, to the gestures associated with particular emotions, or to cultural norms, rather than being from a more ancient system of honest biological signals?

The first thing to note is that most of our experiments involved young and old, male and female, and Asian, Latin, and European nationals going about their day-to-day business. Some of the interactions were even in the subjects' native language rather than in English. Some of the tasks had fixed content, and others were completely free-form. This is not evidence based on U.S. college kids filling out questionnaires.

Further, few of the experiments had an emotional aspect; most involved tasks that the subjects had done hundreds of times and often nothing great was riding on this particular interaction. Moreover, when we asked for subjective judgments we found no significant correlations except for those questions that concerned the social relationship—measures such as empathy, determination, attention, and interest. There is no reason to expect that emotion played a role in these results.

Of course, honest signals are using the same final common path as language, emotional displays, and culturally defined gestures; after all, we only have one voice, one pair of hands, and one face. But honest signals are separate from these other modes of expression in terms of their time course, being much slower than words or even sentences. It typically takes people thirty seconds or more to read other people in social science experiments, for instance.[12] Similarly, it takes around thirty seconds for the sociometer to read social signals, because it takes this long to get enough examples of speaking and gesturing to measure the signals.[13] As a consequence of having different time scales, you can have virtually any combination of words or gestures with virtually any combination of honest signals. They are really quite separate channels of communication.

Because this unconscious, independent channel of communication accurately predicts objective behavior and subjective social impressions, it seems hard to avoid the conclusion that our conscious minds are not fully in control of our behavior. Conscious and unconscious appear to be intertwined in our daily lives, and it is not clear whether the majority of our behavior is driven by this ancient system of honest signals or by our conscious minds. While it is clear that conscious thought can (usually) override our instincts, only a minority of human behaviors may be governed by conscious, cognitive processes.[14]

Elevating the importance of our ancient social senses relative to our conscious mind feels dangerous to some people, as if we were admitting that we are ruled by some base animal nature. The data do not support such a negative view. Instead, they emphasize that our behavior is deeply and immediately connected with that of other humans.

NEXT STEPS

We have seen that honest signals combine to characterize social roles such as leading, teaming, listening, and exploring. These social roles communicate the speaker's social attitude and intent, and are accurate predictors of the interaction outcome. In fact, the signaling that a person displays often has a bigger effect than any other factor.

It is hard to consciously fake these signals, thereby falsely communicating your attitude or intention. Method acting does appear to work, however, if you really, fully put yourself into a particular social role. Whether it is as the leader, the team member, or another role, we find that your signaling automatically and unconsciously changes to match. The fact that you can mentally "put on" different social roles and have your signaling follow suit means that we can change our unconscious communications. Doctors, for instance, are using method acting to improve their unconscious signaling of attention and empathy, and hence, to improve patient care as well as reduce lawsuits.[15]

To exploit this social learning possibility, we have begun building *social prostheses* that help people mold their signaling, so that they can be more socially adept. The basic elements of these social prostheses are a sociometer, to read the signals, and then an interface, to give the user feedback about how they are doing. We have experimented with interfaces such as cell phones, computers, and small earbud audio headsets. Some of the more interesting examples of these social systems are the "jerk-o-meter," which reminds husbands to pay attention to their wives, and the negotiometer, which gives real-time feedback during a negotiation.[16]

The ability to dramatically change people's behavior by the role you adopt and the social signals you display raises some questions: Where is the conscious mind in all this? And what about language? Could this all be some side effect of normal conversation? In the next chapter, we will see that this channel of social communication is parallel, and largely independent of our linguistic and conscious communication. It is an ancient communication channel, possibly one used by our ancestors before the evolution of language.

READING PEOPLE

Imagine, for a moment, that you are playing in a high-stakes poker game. After studying the cards in your hand, you turn to study the players at the table. Glancing at the woman next to you, you notice that she shifts slightly in her chair and adds a little extra energy as she puts down the cards. The player across the table, however, is being just a bit too still. Even his eyes aren't blinking as much as is normal. You decide that the woman next to you must have a good hand, and that the man across the table is bluffing. You place your bet accordingly.

The game of poker revolves around being able to read people and keeping others from reading you. A world-class poker game is an intense social experience rather than a competition between robot-like calculating machines. Poker players focus intently on their opponents for subtle signs of excitement or stress, looking for clues to predict their next move. And they try to monitor their own behaviors to prevent others from detecting the same changes. It's all about observing, understanding, and interpreting unspoken social signals.

The flow of subtle social signals that influences other players' actions forms a web of signals and responses that allows the best players to predict how the game will turn out just by watching the behavior of the other players. But as it turns out, being a human sociometer is extremely difficult, and even professional poker players give away clues about their cards, as mentioned earlier. Remember the player who seemed just a bit too still? We found the same type of signal suppression when we looked at semiprofessional poker games. Players who showed almost no normal signaling were likely to be either bluffing or engaged in some other high-risk play.[1] It is difficult to suppress this automatic, unspoken channel of communication because it is at the core of so much of what we do. When we try to suppress our signaling, it takes a great deal of training to avoid having the suppressed activity "leak out" as small nervous behaviors, and even experts generally overdo it and appear unnaturally quiet.

Just as in a poker game, we are continually immersed in a network of social signals during our daily lives. The constant demands of reading and responding to these signals require enormous energy. As with our other senses, we are largely unaware of this virtuoso performance. All that usually reaches our conscious mind are impressions of attention, determination, supportiveness, and the like. But with practice, we can learn to notice these signals, and that is the difference between the winning poker player and the loser.

TACTICAL ACTION

Card games suggest a model for how our conscious mind fits together with our ancestral social signaling mechanism. The key point is that experienced players have learned the game so well that deciding which card to play in a particular situation has become an almost automatic reflex. For them, once they know what the situation is—which cards have been drawn and so forth—then deciding what to do next is just a matter of reading the social signaling.

The same type of decision making makes an interesting model for how ape troops coordinate their activities. Without language, what do they do? The first point to notice is that apes are good at teamwork. Field research has shown that they are quite effective at exploring and exploiting food resources as well as protecting the troop's territory.[2] The second point is that they use social signaling instead of language to coordinate group behavior.[3]

As a consequence, their group behavior is similar to a long-practiced card game, where deciding what to do next is just a matter of figuring out the physical situation and then reading the social situation. So if you were watching an ape troop going about a familiar activity, then you could just read the social signaling to accurately predict what will happen next. And primatologists can do just that.[4] Our sociometer data tell us that the same is true of people: usually you can just read the social signaling to accurately predict what will happen next.[5] Moreover, social signaling is not only a good predictor of outcomes for impulse decisions or incidental actions such as which seat to choose. Surprisingly, predictions based only on social signaling are also accurate for careful, conscious decisions and even decisions that most would consider good examples of rational thinking. When we watch people within a fixed context, be it salary negotiations, sales pitches, or at dating events, the social signaling is able to predict how things will turn out.

What we have to understand is how the effort we put into marshaling facts, collecting arguments, considering choices, and refining our personal characteristics all averages out to the same set of choices, leaving social signaling as a good predictor of outcomes. To investigate this conundrum, let's return to our card game again. Expert card play requires three things: familiarity with the possible plays and sequences of plays (strategy), the ability to estimate the odds of various sequences of card draws (experience), and the ability to choose a play based on reading the signals of the other players (tactics).

Prediction of the players' actions just from the measurement of social signals is possible *only* in games where the strategic options are fixed and everyone is experienced, so that it is only the tactics that determine the play. Consequently, the fact that social signals are good predictors must mean our subjects were familiar with the range of strategies and how they typically play out. This "ceiling effect" across conscious strategic options seems the most likely way to explain the observed fact that all the scheming and planning we do to approach these decision points is no more predictive than the signaling we display.

How might this ceiling effect have come about? One part of the answer may be that we are strongly bound by our culture, with most of our conscious behavior learned implicitly by observing other people.[6] When behaviors are learned through copying others, then of course they will tend to be the same across different people. A second part of the answer may be that we are all so experienced at situations like dating, negotiation, and teaming that the performance differences between people are small.

This seems to be the case for expert card players, for instance. Few players can actually calculate the odds of certain card combinations or estimate the exact probabilities of sequences of play. Instead, they have enough experience with the game that they have a feel for what to play next; expert players possess a good, qualitative model of the risks and likely outcomes, but one that is implicit and unconscious so that they can't express it precisely through language.

Just because unconscious signaling predicts outcomes, however, doesn't necessarily rule out the involvement of conscious thought. Our behavior could still be driven by the conscious mind, but with the unconscious channel leaking out our decisions for everyone to see. Yet it seems likely that the situation is more complex than having either the conscious or unconscious mind being in complete command. Certain sorts of teasing or ironic humor, for instance, seem to arise from the conscious opposition of signaling and language; consider a young woman saying to a young man "no, I'm not attracted to you" when she knows that he can easily sense her interest from her signaling.

SOCIAL CIRCUITS

Recent studies of the human brain show that we all have *networking hardware* that gives us the ability to instantly read and respond to other people. The key components of this networking hardware are *mirror neurons*, which provide a reading of other people's actions directly to various parts of our brain.[7] These mirror neurons allow us to unconsciously synchronize gestures and match vocal pitch, automatically respond to laughter and smiles, dance and sing together, and more generally coordinate our actions with those of other people.[8]

This same networking hardware supplies us with a direct neural path for reading the honest signals provided by influence, mimicry, activity, and consistent emphasis, and thus allows us to automatically and unconsciously read other people's level of interest, determination, empathy, and the like. As a result, our brains' networking hardware prepares us for coordination in domains beyond music and dance—such as hunters chasing prey, gatherers searching for food, and even white-collar employees working in a team.

This social sense is central to the way our minds develop and how we construct meaning. People use these reactions to unconsciously read social properties such as dominance, attraction, interest, and deception. Infants' development depends critically on the synchrony with and reactions of their mother;[9] childhood learning of social skills is built on mimicry and the social signaling of peers, and even adult acquisition of job skills is heavily dependent on this sort of tacit learning.[10]

Because people have this capability for automatic signaling and response, the signaling of each person can propagate through the chains of people that make up their social network, eventually changing the behavior of the entire group. So when a group of people gets together, we need to consider not just the individual behaviors but also the *social circuits* formed by the patterns of signaling between them. These social circuits specify networks of dominance, obligation, friendliness, attention, and receptivity, which in turn coordinate the day-to-day behavior of the group.

A classic example of social circuits at work is found in mood contagion.[11] Having even a single irrepressibly bubbly, excited person on the team can lift everyone's energy level. Infectious enthusiasm spreads unconsciously through mimicry. This contagion process also has feedback—one person's rising excitement will tend to raise your level of excitement as well. When one person mimics the excited behavior of another, that person will unconsciously begin to be more excited themselves through feedback from their muscular, visceral, and glandular responses. Similarly, as an entire team interacts, the circuits of mimicry can spread this excitement to everyone. The process can go the other way, of course; a depressed person can drag down the whole team.

The phenomenon of charisma may be the most striking example of our social circuitry influencing group behavior.[12] Judgments of charisma are shared across people, showing that the experience of charisma has an objective basis, and charisma is recognized as a key element in social change. And yet we have little or no understanding of the phenomenon, only a definition: charismatic people are unusually expressive, sensitive, and have strong internal control.

Perhaps the best theory so far is that charismatic people are those who are particularly talented at reading and responding to social signaling.[13] We have seen that success at activities where charisma counts—pitching business plans, closing sales, getting hired, and getting a date—are very strongly connected to our ability to read and respond to social signaling. If it turns out that charisma has such deep biological roots, it might even be that charisma is the other end of the autistic spectrum: a genetic variation that affects the ability to read and display social signals, and that is more associated with males than females.[14]

SIGNALS CHANGE PEOPLE

It is tempting to imagine that these social signals are some sort of magic incantation that you can use to control people. But there is a fundamental difference between honest signaling and the more familiar medium of language: signaling inherently changes both people, whereas conscious language can be strictly one-way. When you engage in social signaling, you are often affected just as much as the other person. Signals are two-way, not one-way, communication, so that pulling on one corner of the social fabric stretches all members of the network.

For instance, in the Stanford University experiment discussed above that used a computer-animated sales agent to mimic people, researchers found that mimicry makes the agent seem both more honest and more persuasive.[15] The interesting thing is that this is only half of the story: when someone mimics you, there is a very strong tendency for you to begin mimicking them. This creates a sort of social circuit that reinforces itself, producing a pair of people deeply engaged in mimicking each other, and each feeling better and better about the other person.[16]

This happens in the real world, too. When we looked at salary negotiation, a situation that is prone to distrust and conflict, we found that when one person began mimicking, the other person joined in three-quarters of the time. Furthermore, the amount of mimicking was strongly correlated with feelings of trust.[17] So the consequence is that by mimicking the other person, you can get them to trust you more—but *you* will end up trusting them more as well.[18]

This strange effect of "self-inflicted brainwashing" works even in the simplest situations. When experimenters ask people to move their heads up and down while listening to a sales pitch or seeing a consumer product, the people end up liking the pitch or product more, and they are more likely to buy it. It is as if your brain thinks to itself, "Well, I see that I'm nodding my head, so I guess I must really like this!" Yes, we humans seem to be just this simple.[19]

SOUL LAID BARE

What the sociometer shows us is that our goals, plans, relationships, and intentions are reliably recognizable from simple, unconscious social signals. Finding a mate, getting a job, and making money are some of the most significant tasks in human life, and our subjects had honed these skills for decades. And yet, the unconscious social signaling accurately predicted what they were going to choose and how the interactions were going to turn out.

In well-studied activities where we can compare the importance of social signaling to other factors—activities like negotiation, dating, and sales—the social signaling predicts outcomes better than strategy, motivation, experience, or personal characteristics. We seem to respond to these signals automatically, and the social circuits formed by the patterns of signal and response work to combine our individual desires into a consistent social fabric.

The predictive power of these social signals as measured by the sociometer, moreover, is surprisingly uniform across different situations. In each case, about 40 percent of the variation in behavior can be predicted by the social signaling, regardless of the words used or personal attributes. To put this in context, that is the same as the percentage of personal characteristics that can be attributed to your genetic makeup.

If you use these signals to predict behaviors (and make the call only when you are sure), you can sometimes get as high as 95 percent accuracy at predicting what people are going to do. And by adjusting for personal characteristics and the history of previous interactions, we can dramatically increase our ability to predict people's behavior even when we are forced to predict the outcome of every interaction.

So what should we conclude about people based on the power these basic social signals hold for us? Perhaps humans should be viewed primarily as social animals, where individuals are best likened to musicians in a jazz quartet. Of course we can predict the behavior of these individuals from that of their associates: they are so focused on the group's overall performance and so sensitive to complementing the others in the group that they almost cease to be individuals at all. What the sociometer tells us is that this immersion of self in the surrounding social network is the *typical* human condition, rather than being isolated examples found in exceptional circumstances.

NEXT STEPS

We have seen that social signals combine into social roles, and that these roles form an independent and powerful channel of communication that is separate from the more familiar channel of conscious linguistic communication. This signal-response channel seems to have evolved much earlier than the linguistic channel, with language building on top of the capabilities of this channel.

Social signals also have different properties than the linguistic channel, being inherently two-way rather than one-way communication, so that they work to stitch groups of humans into tightly coupled units. As an example, if you consciously choose to "play" the role of teaming, you are more likely to unconsciously mimic others, which unconsciously increases your trust of them along with the likelihood that you will do business with them. Playing the role of a team member can tighten the bonds within the team and make it work more smoothly, and at the same time make you feel like more of a team member.

So far most of our data have been from pairs of people, not from groups or networks of people. The natural question to ask, then, is how does social signaling work in groups or in larger social networks?

What we will see in the next chapter is that the signals themselves seem to remain unaltered, but that the pattern of signal-response communication that we have found between pairs of people in our previous experiments now becomes dependent on the signaling of the other people in the group. Broadly viewed, honest signals function to bring together individuals in competitive conditions. Although we typically think of that as being a relatively long-term competition (say, for a mate), it appears that honest signals can also serve to bring together people from competing coalitions in a group discussion, despite the fact that these coalitions shift membership and topic quite rapidly.

SURVIVAL SIGNALS

We humans are fascinated with ourselves. There may be little we like to do more than watch other people (except perhaps to gossip about them). We love to observe people around us, and then analyze their behaviors and speculate about their motivations. Just take a look at the magazine covers at your local grocery store if you need confirmation of this tendency. Or consider some of the most popular U.S. television shows of the past few years, shows such as *Survivor* or *The Apprentice*.

Survivor is a particularly good example of our fascination with human behavior and finding the meaning in it. If you have seen the television show, you have probably not watched it in order to learn how to live on your own in the Australian outback or a Central American rain forest; you have watched it in order to soak in the group dynamics on display. Even the participants themselves can't resist it. After a hard day of trying to figure out survival skills in a new environment, do they immediately fall asleep? Do they share tips on finding food or building shelters? No, they usually lie awake whispering to each other about who did what to whom and why. We live in a human sea of social signaling, and spend an enormous amount of our time and brainpower plumbing its depths for information.

Reality television shows were not the first to realize that powerful group dynamics are on display in a survival situation. In fact, simulations of survival situations have been used for years in experimental and social psychology in order to study small group decision-making processes. Within each of these constructed survival situations, we can detect several fundamental truths about human social signaling in groups.

Groups working together add new dimensions to the social signaling present in one-on-one situations. Unlike trying to find a partner through speed dating or negotiating a raise with your boss, these group situations contain competing coalitions supporting different alternatives, with the membership of the coalitions shifting as different tasks and ideas are introduced. This added layer of complexity in groups challenges us to examine how honest signals work to coordinate individual behavior in the midst of group competition.

Whether you are part of a team developing a business plan or trying to survive in the rain forest, you and your social role and signaling are part of a continuous loop connected to the social world around you. The social role assumed by any given individual is determined in part by that person, but also by the other people in the group who are interacting with that individual. To further complicate matters, the participants in a group decision-making process may take on many different roles, each with its own characteristic signaling display. Again, we will see the value of honest signals in explaining this exquisite social dance executed within every group.

SOCIAL ROLES IN GROUPS

Almost half a century ago, the U.S. National Aeronautics and Space Administration developed a team exercise called "survival" to help train people to work together and help social scientists better understand decision making under stress.[1] Each small team is given the imaginary situation of being stranded in a remote location such as the Canadian north woods, and then asked to decide what items are going to be most important in helping them to survive. The survival exercise has remained popular in social science because this consensus decision-making scenario produces intensive engagement, and creates a wide range of social dynamics and attitudes.

Social scientists traditionally analyze the members of a survival team in terms of their group role (e.g., attacker, neutral, protagonist, or supporter) and task role (e.g., giver, seeker, neutral, or orienteer).[2] Although the labels may be unfamiliar, we are all intimately familiar with these roles because we have played them hundreds of times in our daily lives. One taxonomy of these group and task roles (a version of Robert Bales's Interaction Process Analysis)[3] can be summarized as in the table below.

GROUP ROLES

Attacker: Deflates the status of others, expresses disapproval, and attacks the group or the problem

Protagonist: Takes the floor, drives the conversation, assumes a personal perspective, and asserts authority

Supporter: Shows a cooperative attitude demonstrating understanding, attention, and acceptance as well as providing technical and relational support

Neutral: Passively accepts the idea of others, serving as an audience in group discussion

TASK ROLES

Orienteer: Orients the group by introducing the agenda, defining goals and procedures, keeping the group focused and on track, and summarizing the most important arguments and the group decisions

Giver: Provides factual information and answers to questions, states beliefs and attitudes about an idea, and expresses personal values and factual information

Seeker: Requests suggestions and information as well as clarifications to promote effective group decisions

Follower: Listens without actively participating in the interaction

The group and task roles are seen as being different and complementary dimensions of group behavior.

This traditional approach to role classification has some real ability to predict the outcome of group decision making. For instance, researchers have found that certain abnormal patterns in task and group roles are associated with poor group decision making, including familiar problems such as groupthink and polarization.[4] If there are two or more people taking the attacker role, say, more extreme, polarized decisions tend to result. If there is only one protagonist and everyone else is a supporter, a typical outcome is groupthink, where group members just follow the leader without exploring the whole range of options and dangers.

Despite its predictive value, this sort of task/group analysis is almost never used in real life. This is because it is difficult and expensive to use; it requires a trained psychologist to go through a videotape of the interaction second by second, carefully labeling each interaction. The laborious nature of the processing also limits its usefulness in another way, as it is not feasible to utilize this approach to give live feedback.

But what if we could do this sort of analysis based on measures of the group's honest signaling? What if the group and task roles were in fact closely related to the social roles we see when we measure people's signaling in other situations? If so, then we could use the sociometer to build real-time computer systems that give feedback to the group, and predict which interactions are likely to be successful and which are likely to be disastrous.

In the next section, we will see that these traditional ways of analyzing group interactions can be done automatically, by using a computer algorithm that builds on the sociometer's ability to read the group's honest signaling. Using this technology we are beginning to build real-time meeting management tools that help keep groups on track, by providing them with feedback to help avoid problems like groupthink and polarization.

HONEST SIGNALS IN GROUPS

To understand more about the general relationship between honest signals and group behavior, we examined data from a set of survival exercises conducted by Massimo Zancanaro's research group in Trento, Italy.[5] They videotaped twelve groups of four people deciding how to survive a plane crash in a snowy northern forest, and used cameras and microphones to measure each person's speaking activity level, body and hand gestures, and engagement with others. In addition, trained observers labeled every part of the decision-making process, using the traditional-style task and group roles.

When we used the sociometer methodology to examine these survival exercises, our first surprise was that analyzing the unconscious social signaling from a thirty-second "thin slice" of behavior yielded a good guess about what group and task roles a person was performing.[6] And this was accomplished without examining any words, the order of speaking, or even what the participants were speaking about. The signaling alone told the story.

Social signaling	Exploring	Teaming	Active listening	Leading
Group role	Protagonist	Supporter	Neutral	Attacker
Task role	Giver	Orienteer	Follower	

Whenever a person adopted a different group or task role, we found that they also changed their unconscious social signaling to match the role. As a consequence, you could figure out what role they were playing by just measuring their social signaling with a sociometer. As shown in the table above, people playing the pro-tagonist role were typically displaying the exploring signaling we found in social networking and dating. People in the supporter role were typically displaying the teaming signaling we found in successful salary negotiations and job interviews. Neutrals displayed active listening signals. And when people took on the role of attacker, they displayed strong leading signals.

Moreover, the group and task roles were not really separate from each other. People in fact played particular group roles depending on which task they were carrying out. Our sociometer data showed that protagonists played the task role of givers, supporters played the task role of orienteers, and neutrals were followers.

Our sociometer-based labeling of group and task roles, however, wasn't as accurate as the human experts until we took *social context* into account. When we looked at *everyone's* signaling during a thirty-second slice of the exercise, then the sociometer readings could label the roles as accurately as the human experts (although the pattern of labeling errors was different). An accurate reading of a person's group or task role depends not only on the individual's unconscious signaling but also on the signaling of others. Roles are best read from the social circuits, rather than from the signaling of individuals.

So simply by observing the pattern of unconscious social signaling, you can figure out a lot about the group's dynamics. You can, for instance, detect when the group is moving toward problems like groupthink or polarization. Just as in the one-on-one case, language and argument matter, but sometimes they matter surprisingly little.

An intriguing interpretation of these results is that much of the group behavior we attribute to conscious decision and argument might have developed from ancient patterns of unconscious signaling and role taking. Although our conscious and unconscious communication channels are likely to be completely enmeshed and intertwined, it might be that the dynamics of group interaction are still grounded on unconscious signal-response behavior. That is, perhaps the function of our conscious role taking, strategy, and argument is to elaborate a pattern of interaction that is established by our unconscious social circuitry.

There are several suggestive hints that our unconscious social circuitry plays a central role within group dynamics. One particularly telling observation is that when a group is deciding among different alternatives, you can often predict which choice the group will select by simply paying attention to the initial reactions. The group's behavior is frequently almost like voting: the alternative with the largest number of positive initial comments is usually the winner.[7] Furthermore, you can see this "prediction by initial reaction" effect using the sociometer: not only can you measure individual interest from individual signaling behavior,[8] but you can also measure the group's interest from the members' combined signaling behavior.[9] It is surprising that the group discussion makes so little difference, and that this sort of "first-reaction" social signaling predicts the outcome so well. Just as in our studies of negotiation or poker, all that hard conscious work doesn't seem to make as much difference as we might expect.

Another observation supporting the centrality of unconscious social circuitry in groups comes from studies of brainstorming sessions. In this case, the average activity level in a brainstorming group is predictive of the *productivity* of the group.[10] That is, quiet groups are no more productive than having their members brainstorm separately, but highly active, engaged groups are more productive than the sum of their parts. This seems to be because the average level of interest within a group is closely related to the average activity level of the group, as would be expected from the relationship between activity and individual interest we have found in simpler situations.[11] More active groups may simply be groups where the participants are more interested and hence more productive.

In previous chapters we have seen that individual decision making can be predicted by unconscious social signaling, and now we have seen strong connections between unconscious social circuitry and outcomes in group decision making. The specific patterns of social signaling associated with task and group roles in the survival experiments, the first-reaction votelike signaling observed during group decision making and the active, engaged signaling seen during group brainstorming point to the significance of unconscious social circuitry in group dynamics.

VIBES AND BUZZ

Our negotiation data demonstrated how people's signaling was often answered by similar signaling, which suggests how social roles such as teaming or exploring can spread throughout a group. For instance, in productive brainstorming groups the signaling of interest and attention seems to reinforce itself through feedback from others.[12] As people become infected with enthusiasm from other group members, better results are obtained.

Enthusiasm is not the only thing that can be spread by social circuits. Attitudes such as trust, openness, and identification with the team can also spread though teaming, listening, and exploring behaviors.[13]

Perhaps this is why venture capitalists frequently rate start-up firms by the buzz and feel that they have. They ask questions such as: Is the team energetic and engaged? Is there a high level of trust and openness? Is there a strong feeling of team and membership? These characteristics of a start-up's social network are exactly those created, spread, and maintained by social circuitry.[14] The reason venture capitalists assess these social network properties is that together they determine key aspects of the organization's intelligence: its capacity to reason, plan, solve problems, and learn.[15]

Indeed, venture capitalists are correct to focus on these social network attributes; group attitudes, of course, can have enormous effects on the performance of the group. And we humans tend to quickly take on the attitude of a group when we are immersed in a new social context. This process of attitude change through immersion can be negative as well as positive, however. One need only think of Stanley Milgram's experiments,[16] in which social circuitry between experimenters and naive subjects was used to manipulate subjects into (apparently) harming other people, or Phil Zimbardo's Stanford Prison Experiment,[17] in which social circuitry subverted university students into acting like violent prison guards, to appreciate the speed and power of social circuits to spread attitudes throughout a group.

Because of this power of social circuits to unconsciously influence group attitudes, people sometimes design meetings to purposely minimize their effect. Although gatherings that short-circuit the social signaling, such as international trade negotiations, may be largely immune to the unconscious social pressures that can be caused by social signaling, they are also famously plodding and unproductive. If you go to a session at the United Nations, say, you will see each person present written speeches in a designated order, and most people listen to a translator rather than the speaker themselves. The result is that while influence due to signaling has been reduced to near zero, the experience is also terminally boring.

NEXT STEPS

Honest signals have evolved to coordinate individual behaviors in the midst of competition. In groups, though, competition is not just a one-on-one situation. There are instead competing coalitions supporting different alternatives, with the membership of the coalition shifting with each different question or new idea. Consequently, participants take on many different roles in quick succession, each with its own characteristic signaling display.

Evolution seems to have equipped our signal-response system to be able to handle this shifting competition, allowing role-based signaling to help bring together competing groups. In a group situation, the role you assume (and the signaling that goes with it) is no longer a function of one other person, but rather is a function of the signaling of the entire group.

An important finding was that we could use the social signaling to accurately determine each person's group and task roles. This means that we can build on sociometer readings to create a computerized feedback system that helps groups steer away from groupthink and polarization. Early experiments with this sort of real-time "meeting mediator" are already providing promising results.[8]

Perhaps the most significant observation was that in the survival experiment data, the pattern of role taking was similar across all the participants as well as across all the topics and discussions. That is, the network of social circuits within these groups did *not* depend on either the content of the discussion or the particular individuals involved. Rather, the role taking and social circuitry seemed to create a sort of decision-making machine, which draws out ideas from individuals and "processes" them until one is selected as the group's decision.

This raises an obvious question: Does role-taking behavior really produce a decision-making machine? Is there a theory of how this sort of signaling machine works to produce good decisions? And how can it do this without knowing anything about the content of the discussion? The answers to these questions will form a theory of rational decision making that is different from the one we have inherited from the Greeks and Enlightenment philosophers. Instead of rationality based on the syllogism, logic, and argument, we will see rationality based on minimizing risk and maximizing reward. Our ability to make group decisions may have evolved from an ancient signaling mechanism that is based on a market of ideas rather than on deduction.

NETWORK INTELLIGENCE

It is evening in prehistoric Africa. After a day of gathering and hunting, the young adults have returned to share food, groom each other, and recount the events and observations of the day. They have no sophisticated language ability, so the communication is through pantomime, gesture, and a few concrete nouns and verbs. During this group "discussion," social signaling—the tone of voice, laughter, body posture, gesture, and so forth—reflects each individual's desires and interests in the topics raised, and reaffirms their position in the social life of the tribe. This signaling accompanies each discussion item, and the collective social signaling communicates the group's reaction back to each member of the tribe: Is this item new and interesting? Is it important? Does it endanger someone's vested interest? Does it open up new opportunities for someone? In the end, collective decisions have been made and everyone knows what duties to perform during the next day, not because of any explicit declaration, but because each individual has read the sense of the group.

But how did primitive humans make group decisions? With only limited language skills, the decision process couldn't really involve logical argument. For that matter, how do ape groups decide what to do? With language removed from the equation, some way must still exist to gather and assess the possibilities for group action, and make group decisions that maximize rewards and minimize risk. There also has to be a way for each individual to know what the group decided, so that everyone can play their respective roles.

Clearly, we need a solid, working explanation of how prelinguistic communication, including social signaling, could produce intelligent, coordinated group behavior in early humans. Studies of primitive human groups reinforce the idea that social interactions are central to human decision making; ethologists have found that almost all decisions affecting the group as a whole are made in social situations.[1] The major exception to this pattern of social decision making, in humans as well as other animals, is when extremely rapid decision making is required for situations such as battles or emergencies.[2]

In our close cousins the apes, whose only known communication is nonlinguistic, decision making via the use of social signaling is a familiar scenario. For instance, Kelly Stewart and Alexander Harcourt report that mountain gorillas decide when to end an afternoon siesta by using "close call" signals.[3] When everyone in the group has been heard from, and the "conversation" reaches a certain intensity level, then the rest period is over. Similarly, Sue Boinski and Aimee Campbell describe how capuchin monkeys use trilling sounds to cooperatively decide when and where the troop should move.[4] Monkeys at the leading edge of the troop trill the most, encouraging others to follow the path they have found, and others take up the trilling in order to coordinate everyone's movements.

Similar patterns of social decision making are common in many animals and virtually all primates. The signaling mechanism varies, from vocalization to body posture to head movements, but the structure of the decision-making process remains pretty much the same: cycles of signaling and recruitment, until a point is reached where everyone in the group accepts that a consensus has been reached.[5] Some evolutionary theorists think that this type of "social voting" process could be the most common type of decision making for social animals, in part because it is good at accounting for the cost-benefit trade-offs of everyone in the group. In addition, this type of consensus process typically avoids extreme decisions, making it more likely that the entire group will follow the decision.

But the fact that social signals are commonly used to make group decisions doesn't explain *how* social decision making can produce successful, adaptive behavior. We still need a good explanation of how social signaling mechanisms can produce *intelligent* decisions.

IDEA MARKETS: HARNESSING THE POWER OF THE GROUP

The most interesting property of socially mediated group decision making is that an effective group can potentially be *smarter than any of its individual members*. This power stems from the group's potential to accurately integrate information gathered by many different members. The idea that groups can be smarter than an isolated individual is an old one—it is why we gather in groups to brainstorm and make decisions, after all—but it is receiving new interest now that modern telecommunications have made it common to have work groups that are spread all around the world.

Over one hundred years ago in Victorian England, the Reverend Thomas Bayes developed a mathematical theory for combining information. His theory shows how to weight bits of information in proportion to their expected payoff in order to make the best possible overall prediction. In other words, the Bayesian approach can produce decisions that maximize the expected return and minimize the risk.

Idea markets built on this Bayesian solution for combining information are an effective way to integrate people's opinions.[6] One key difference between voting and an idea market is that instead of a single vote per person, we allow people to express their expectation of the return associated with each course of action. For instance, how much food will we find if we go over the hill? How much will we find if we go across the river? And so forth for each alternative. For convenience, we will refer to these opinions as *bets*, since they are after all expectations about the payoff.

What sort of signaling and group interaction would create a working idea market in modern organizations? The previous chapter provided a hint at how this might be accomplished. As you will recall, social scientists have long known that when new proposals are introduced to a group, there is typically a series of positive and negative initial reactions. Although traditional social scientists have focused mostly on the linguistic content of the initial reaction comments,[7] there is also a layer of unconscious signaling that complements this conscious level of communication.[8] These initial reactions are a good prediction of the final group decision, so just as with the social signaling experiments in earlier chapters, all the discussion and strategizing often makes little difference in the final outcome.

Thinking back to our poker game example, we can see that the predictive power of initial signaling makes sense. If we imagine young children playing cards, we would expect that each time a card was placed face up, the signaling accompanying the card would be a direct indication of its anticipated payoff. Cards that are helpful would be met with choruses of "all right!" and "high fives!" (high activity and mimicry), whereas disappointing cards would produce slumped bodies and groans (low activity and high variability/low consistency). The signaling shown by adults is suppressed and thus much more difficult to read, but it is still the same.

This initial reaction signaling contains the building blocks for an idea market. Each person's signaling of interest reflects their estimate of their personal payoff, and the proposal with the most support across the entire group wins. So it is easy to create an idea market using social signaling: everyone bets on each suggested action by adjusting their activity level (signaling interest), and then we just add up the total amount of activity in the group and pick the alternative with the most bets.

Selecting a course of action by comparing the "activation level" associated with each alternative is similar to theories of how our brain makes decisions. Instead of a neural network selecting the action with the most neural activation, however, here we are selecting the alternative that produces the greatest activation of the social network. This similarity between neural networks and social networks is discussed further in appendix E.

Decision making by using social signals to create an idea market isn't based on logic or argument; it is based on Bayes's mathematics. In fact, this method of decision making has no need for language beyond signs for the proposed actions and goals. In order to pick the winning course of action, each person must be able to signal to the group how interested they are in each alternative and then be able to read the combined signaling of the group. This is what seems to be going on in our example of apes deciding which way to go, and it is similar to the initial reaction signaling that psychologists see in modern business meetings.

Because this method involves reading the social network to make decisions and predictions, I have dubbed it network intelligence. The process of reading the social network is simply observing and absorbing the social signaling that occurs around a question in order to harvest the network's decision-making power. The key difference between network intelligence and most theories of human behavior is the critical role that unconscious social signals and responses play in fusing the mental capabilities of individuals into an effective decision-making capability.

IDIOTS AND GOSSIP

Unfortunately, this simple type of group decision-making process works well for only some concerns. To be reliably better than individuals across many types of issues, we have to be careful to avoid two fundamental problems: idiots and gossip.

The problem of idiots is easy to solve: you just have to account for people who aren't good at predicting the outcome of actions. To do this, you have to weight people's opinion by their track record at estimating payoffs in previous decisions. This weighting, when done properly, takes care of the problem of idiots.

The problem of gossip is much harder. Bayes assumed that each bit of information was *independent*, so that you could count each bit of information exactly once. Unfortunately, the information available to people often comes from shared sources, and then people go on to discuss the information and shape each other's opinions. The betting patterns of people are therefore frequently similar, which is the opposite of what is required. Failures in group decision making, including phenomena like groupthink and polarization, are at their heart a failure to take full account of which bits of information are independent and which are copies propagated through the social network; the result is that information is aggregated inappropriately.[9]

There are three basic ways to deal with this problem. The first method might be called the *bookie* solution to the problem of gossip. Bernardo Huberman's research group at Hewlett-Packard developed a scheme that first asked each person to bet on what everyone else was going to say.[10] This "common knowledge" was then discounted, since it was obviously being counted more than once. Already several companies, including Intel and Hewlett-Packard, are making use of this sort of mathematically corrected market mechanism—essentially structured betting—to aggregate pricing information across their employees. This strategy is making tens of millions of dollars per month by making better price and demand predictions than established trading experts—proof of the power of idea markets that have addressed the problems of idiots and gossip.

While it is useful for some situations, the bookie method doesn't work well for predicting subjective outcomes such as which movie people will like best. To tackle this problem, Drazen Prelec at MIT came up with what he calls "Bayesian truth serum," which is a way of figuring out who has genuinely new bits of information that might make a difference.¹¹ One might call this the *wise guys* solution to the problem of gossip.

In the wise guys method, you look for individuals who can accurately predict how other people will bet, but whose own bet is different. The logic is that if you can predict other people's bets, then you know the common knowledge. But if your opinion is also different than everyone else's, then you must know something they don't. Your bet, then, can be counted as an independent bit of information.

The difficulty with both the bookie and wise guys methods is that there is little reason to believe that people are good at knowing what other people think, especially in large or distributed organizations. Moreover, they require people to bet on what other people think about each possible alternative—a process that is both time-consuming and likely to be distorted by a whole range of social pressures and subjective mental quirks.

Perhaps the most natural method of dealing with gossip is to extend the idea of network intelligence so that you not only read the signaling around each issue but also keep track of how information flows within the social network. This approach allows you to tease out which opinions are independent of the others so that you don't double count. This more sophisticated version of network intelligence uses knowledge about the network in order to better harvest the network's decision-making power.

To take care of the problem of gossip, you need to know which bits of signaling are independent and which are just "me too" copies. To figure this out, you need to know two things about each pair of people: how similar their bets were in previous idea markets (especially those dealing with related topics), and how much their pattern of communication affects the similarity of their betting. With these two bits of information you can predict how effective their recent interactions will be in shaping each other's opinion, and therefore how independent their betting behavior will be in the current idea market.

The network intelligence method to take care of gossip, therefore, is to discount duplicated opinions in two different ways. First, tight social groups tend to have the same information and the same opinions, so bets from the same social group can't count as independent. Second, people who have previously had similar opinions on other questions probably have similar sources of information, so bets by these birds of a feather can't count as independent either. By paying attention to information flow within the network we can discount these social network effects, allowing us to integrate opinions that are more likely to be truly independent.

TREASURE HUNT

To show how this improved sort of network intelligence works, we constructed a pilot experiment in which six groups of three subjects each wore sociometers while they went on a treasure hunt.[12] The participants were told to look for specially marked images of familiar people, but when they returned we asked them about something else entirely. We asked them about how many people had appeared in the *background* of the target images—something they had not been instructed to notice.

This treasure hunt experiment is similar to a hunting party that is asked about unusual conditions after returning from a hunt, or a management team that is asked to estimate threats and opportunities that are outside of normal operating procedures. Serendipitous information gathering and assessment of this type is often central to strategic planning.

To reach a group decision, we first asked people for *private* bets on how many people had appeared in the background of the target images and then we combined these bets using different versions of network intelligence. First we used the sociometer to measure the actual, *objective* flow of information in order to discount closely related bets, so that we could see how well network intelligence could do under the best possible conditions. We then used our subjects' *subjective* impressions of the flow of information to see how well people did relative to the ideal.

What the data from this experiment showed was that when we aggregated information by taking into account objective social data—the social network structure as measured by the sociometers worn during the treasure hunt—we obtained estimates that were *twice* as accurate as even the best individual estimates and *five* times better than a simple averaging of people's bets. Network intelligence provided by far the best answer.

So can people take advantage of this network intelligence? That is, can we use our talents for tracking social interactions to accurately aggregate information across a group, thereby producing judgments that are more accurate than those of individual humans? Or to phrase it more provocatively, can we humans use our special-purpose "social brain" to produce a superhuman intelligence?

To test this idea, we asked our treasure hunt subjects to use their social brain to tell us how they thought information had spread through the social network. When we again aggregated information across the group, but now using the private, *subjective* estimates of information flow, we got essentially the same estimates as when using *objective* social information. So at least in this simple case, people were able to keep track of the information flow well enough to produce a nearly ideal reading of the network intelligence. The conclusion is that an intelligent reading of the network can produce intelligent decisions. In fact, in this experiment, reading the network intelligence produced as good an answer as we could tease out from the group using state-of-the-art group decision-making methods. As a final exercise, we ran the participants through a carefully structured group decision-making process that allowed each person to see what all of the others thought and then react to their opinions. The result was that the group's final consensus was statistically *identical* to that produced by network intelligence. So instead of engaging in elaborate and time-consuming decision-making exercises, it seems that you may be able to simply read the network intelligence and get to the *same* decision immediately.

MANAGING NETWORK INTELLIGENCE

Thinking back again to young children playing cards, it is easy to imagine that the signaling that accompanies each new card would be a direct indication of their anticipated payoff, because kids aren't good at hiding their interest. In such an open, expressive environment it would be easy to read the network intelligence and predict the likely outcome. With expert players, however, their attempts to hide their interest by suppressing their signaling would make it difficult to "read off" accurate predictions.

Consequently, creating a useful decision process based on signaling requires creating an atmosphere of trust and empathy so that it is easy to read the network. It is interesting to note that the social signals we saw in our survival experiments—mostly exploring and teaming signals—are also the type of signals needed to encourage the sort of open, unguarded signaling that makes an easy-to-read idea market.

This social circuitry also has another important advantage. The exploring and teaming signaling includes high levels of activity, influence, and mimicry. These social signals produce signaling feedback that induces increased interest and engagement by group members as well as increased feelings of trust and empathy. This induction effect causes a virtuous cycle of feedback within the group that increases the cohesion and effectiveness of the group.[13]

This social signaling feedback affects managers as well as team members. Research shows that managers of teams with high levels of interest, engagement, and trust become more integrated into the team, and will operate more democratically. Not surprisingly, these sorts of more egalitarian teams also perform better.[14]

The take-home message for managers is that if you want to make wise decisions, then be sure to spend time reading your organization's network intelligence. Create an open environment through the face-to-face promotion of trust and empathy so that it becomes easy to read the signaling. Spend time reading your group's signaling around each issue, taking care to adjust for the problems of idiots and gossip. By utilizing your group's inherent network intelligence, you can reliably make better decisions than you could on your own.

NEXT STEPS

We have seen that the social roles of teaming, exploring, listening, and leading are conveyed by social signals, and that these signals are powerful predictors of interaction outcomes. We have also seen that social signals are a critical element in shaping how groups of people interact, how the behavior of the group evolves, and even how effective the group is at solving problems.

In this chapter, I have described how the patterns of signaling within a social network can form a machine that decides among alternative actions. It can accomplish this by serving as an idea market, maximizing reward and minimizing risk according to Bayes's formulation.

A careful reading of the signaling within your social network, then—a process that I have named network intelligence—can allow you to integrate information from across the network and make better decisions than you could by yourself. Making this network intelligence work reliably requires discounting signaling from poor-quality sources (idiots) and duplicate signaling (gossip). In addition, it is useful to create an atmosphere of trust and empathy so that it is easy to read the network. By reinforcing this healthy social circuitry and paying close attention to the social network, a leader can harness the network intelligence of the group to improve its decision-making ability.

Network intelligence's need to keep track of all the circuitry in a social network is a huge computational task, yet it is one that humans do almost effortlessly, because our brain's computational engine is specialized for just this sort of social and political thinking. Indeed, Robin Dunbar has collected extensive evidence that the task of understanding interactions within social networks can account almost completely for the rapid expansion of our ancient ancestors' frontal cortex.[15]

The improved decision-making capability offered by network intelligence might also be the basis for the evolution of leadership within human groups. As David Wilson argues, an improvement in decision-making ability that comes from reading the group's social signaling would confer an evolutionary advantage that accrues to the *entire* cultural group, not just to the leader, regardless of the group's genetic heritage.[16]

This evolutionary advantage would result in the selection of the types of network intelligence that produced the most accurate and reliable decision making. As such, the signaling and circuitry that occur in primitive human groups may tell us a great deal about what sorts of group decision making we are naturally good at and how to promote effective decision making in modern-day organizations.

The question for the next chapter is how can this idea of network intelligence be extended beyond small groups to include large organizations and diffuse social networks? Can we harness our innate capabilities for cooperation through social circuitry to build a network intelligence that includes hundreds or even millions of people? One answer is to convert our ancient instinct for verbal grooming—that is, our talent for gossip—into a tool for searching out new information and mobilizing the entire community.

6

SENSIBLE ORGANIZATIONS

Bees do it, ants do it, and perhaps even educated people do it. No, it's not love as Cole Porter imagined it, but something that possibly stymies us more: good group decision making. I have discussed how social signals are a critical element of communication in one-on-one interactions as well as how social signals are important for idea generation and information integration in small groups. Once we remove the problems caused by idiots and gossip, we have also seen how the right kinds of social circuits can create group decisions that are regularly better than individual decisions. But how does this translate to larger groups—modern organizations, for example—where groups are more fluid and electronic communications are a crucial part of the decision-making process? Perhaps bees can give us a clue.

One of the most important group decisions made by a bee colony is where to locate the nest. This particular type of decision making in bees is well studied. The colony sends out a small number of scouts to survey the environment for good nest locations; typically, scouts comprise about 5 percent of the total group. When the scouts return to the colony with information, those who found a more promising site signal their finding by dancing at a higher intensity and for a longer period of time. (Sound familiar? Interest and heightened activity are associated in most animals.)

As a result of this social signaling, more scouts are recruited to the better sites. After additional scouts explore the better sites and return to signal their findings, the dancing of the scouts skews further in favor of the better sites. Eventually so many scouts are signaling in favor of the best site that a tipping point is reached, and the entire colony picks up and moves. Social signaling, communicated by higher activity, causes the information from individual scouts to be communicated, weighted, and pooled, iteratively recruiting a larger and larger fraction of the colony, until a group consensus is reached.[1]

DISCOVERY

The bees' decision-making process highlights information *discovery* as well as information integration. Good group decision making must not only eliminate the problems of idiots and gossip but also the problem of ignorance. How do you know you have found the best location for your nest if you haven't done a thorough survey of the surrounding environment?

The bees' solution to the problem of ignorance seems to be using an idea market to guide discovery, proportionally allocating scouts to the leading ideas after each round of signaling. The use of an idea market to guide discovery is an elegant solution, since it couples the expenditure for exploration to the expected return; it is not so different from what venture capitalists do when they allocate funds for start-ups in proportion to the amount of growth expected in each segment of the economy.

The bees' behavior is strikingly similar to the behavior we think might have been typical of early human groups. A portion of the tribe goes out each day looking—some looking for food to gather, and some looking for good hunting—and at the end of the day they gather around a campfire and integrate their observations using an idea market based on social signaling.[2] The members of the tribe read this network intelligence and decide their actions for the next day. Just as with the bees, the most promising food sources have the most positive signaling behavior and naturally recruit more people. Over a period of days, so many people may be recruited that the entire tribe will decamp to be closer to this abundant food source.

The theory that resource discovery in early human groups was driven by a campfire idea market fits the data we have from the observations of modern tribal groups, although these data are not as detailed as the observations of bee colonies. In virtually every tribal group that has been surveyed, decisions that affect the tribe are made by groups in a social context, accompanied by rich social signaling,[3] and in between these integrative periods the tribe splits up into much smaller groups for resource discovery. This seems so natural to us that we forget that this is not the only way to live; some animals live almost exclusively as herds or hunting packs, and others live as lone individuals meeting with others of their kind only rarely.

The same sort of oscillation between seeking out new information and then integrating it is seen at conferences, where teams of people from the same company spread out to find interesting exhibits, and then regroup and share this new information with the rest of the team.[4] When we asked attendees at two large conferences held within our building to wear sociometers, collecting more than fifteen hundred hours of data from almost two hundred people, we found exactly this pattern of oscillation between discovery and integration. Even though the people came from over fifty different companies, from Asia, the Americas, and Europe, they all showed the same behavior. In fact, we could identify which people were members of the same company with more than 90 percent accuracy simply by looking at which groups of people had identical patterns of oscillation between exploring and integration.

This pattern of information discovery alternating with integration can also be seen in modern corporations, as described by Deborah Ancona and colleagues at MIT when they examined drug discovery teams in pharmaceutical companies.[5] The most productive teams consisted of a core group of tightly connected peers, together with a wide network of affiliates. These productive teams would alternate between integrative meetings of the entire network of individuals and independent exploration where the network of affiliates looked for items of interest to the team. But most of the affiliates weren't part of the formal organization or even given tasks to accomplish. Instead, they noted the areas of interest that came up during the big integration meetings and then used their reading of this network intelligence to guide their independent search. All of this is much like our bees.

NETWORK AND FUNCTION

What bees, early humans, and modern drug discovery groups seem to be doing is using signaling of interest to drive the discovery of information. Individuals read indications of interest within the group (network intelligence) to guide their personal actions, and the result is the gradual recruitment and coordination of the entire group around the best discoveries.

But why does the drive to discover new information and integrate it into the group produce this oscillating social network? Since the classic studies of Alexander Bavelas at MIT nearly sixty years ago, we have known that teams with a centrally coordinated structure—the classic "org chart" structure—are good for fixed, well-defined tasks, but not for complex tasks requiring flexibility.[6] Conversely, teams with richer interconnections are good for tasks requiring flexibility.

Discovery is a task where a centralized structure works well, because the role of the individual is to find and then report information to a central repository, individual, or committee. In contrast, integration and decision making, the sort of information processing that is best handled by an idea market, works best with a fully connected network that allows individuals to hear everyone else's opinion about the expected return for each alternative action. These rich interconnections allow people to change their own bet in response to other people's bets, which results in a more efficient market. Finally, a richly connected network allows everyone to read the network intelligence and conduct themselves accordingly.

The problem is that organizations have to do *both* information discovery and integration, yet these activities work best with different network structures. The solution found by many organisms and human organizations is to alternate between the centralized network that is best for discovery and the richly connected network that is best for integration. By changing network structure over time, sometimes alternating as quickly as every few days, you can shape the overall information flow to suit the different needs of discovery and integration.

Yared Kidane and Peter Gloor at MIT have recently suggested that this sort of oscillation between discovery and integration may be characteristic of creative teams.[7] In collaboration with Gloor and Daniel Oester here at MIT, we asked the marketing division of a German bank to wear sociometers for a period of one month, collecting data from twenty-two employees organized into four teams.[8] When the data were analyzed, we found that the teams charged with creating new marketing campaigns showed an oscillation between the centralized pattern of communication associated with discovery and a densely interconnected pattern of communication where most conversations were with other team members. In contrast, members of production groups showed little oscillation, speaking mostly to other team members.[9]

We discovered a similar connection when we compared teams within the Sloan School of Management and groups within the Media Laboratory using smart phones programmed to perform as sociometers.[10] Members of the Sloan teams were assigned by lottery and were mostly solving class problems. The Media Lab teams were research groups created through interviews and selected for compatibility, and are known for their creativity. Examining 330,000 hours of data from ninety-four people, we found that the Media Lab teams had much more variation in the shape of their social network.

The range of variation in the network shape, moreover, was correlated with how productive the group judged itself to be.

So bees do it, ants do it, and creative teams of people do it too. Oscillation between discovery, characterized by a star-shaped pattern of communication, and integration, characterized by a densely connected pattern of communication, is an incredibly ancient mechanism for combining resource discovery with group decision making.

CONTROLLING THE FLOW OF INFORMATION

What controls the pattern of communication within the social network? Within a face-to-face meeting, attention and interest, signaled by influence on the conversational turn taking and activity level, are critical in shaping the pattern of communication. What the sociometer data show us is that influence and activity also shape people's *overall* pattern of communication—that is, their pattern of who they talk to, when, and in what groupings.

People who are paying attention to each other tend to coordinate their activities (which we can measure as influence), and people who are interested spend more time talking together (a measure of activity). Consequently, people who are working together are more likely to stop to talk in the hall, go for lunch, get coffee, go out for a drink, and so forth, thereby influencing each other's pattern of communication. People who are avoiding each other still coordinate their activity, but it is so that they don't end up meeting in the hall, sitting together at lunch, and so on. This is true even in the smallest activities. For instance, if you watch people walking across a plaza, the amount of influence between two people allows us to accurately tell who is following whom, who is avoiding whom, and who is trying to catch up with whom.[11]

People who have greater influence on the pattern of network connections also have greater power in guiding the information flow. The power a person has over the information flow is often described by their *centrality* within the social network. The mathematical definition of centrality comes from calculating how many paths of information run through the person.[12] These differences in influence make some people more central to the network, and others less central. Influence brings centrality, and centrality brings greater control over the flow of information within the network.

The oscillating pattern of communication we see in bees and humans thus causes oscillating changes in both the centrality of individuals and the average centrality within the group. In traditional organizations the leader of a group is central, since all the information flows through the leader. Similarly, there are some people who act as gateways between different groups. Since the information has to go through them to spread from one group to the other, these people are also central in the network. Members of groups where everyone interacts, by contrast, are less central because the information flows along many different paths.

You can read the information flow within the social network by measuring influence, because there is a very strong relationship between a person's centrality in the network and the amount of influence they have on *both* conversational turn taking and the pattern of communication. For example, in one experiment we asked twenty-five people in several related research groups to wear a sociometer for two weeks and collected over sixteen hundred hours of interaction data. When we later compared people's influence on conversational turn taking with their network centrality, we found an almost mechanical relationship between social signaling and centrality. The more a person influenced the speaking style of everyone they talked with, the more they were central to the social network.[13]

Influence provides an extremely sensitive measure of centrality, and so offers a way to monitor the information flow within an organization. In fact, by using the sociometer to measure the influence between people, we can figure out who are members of the same team or who is the team leader. You can even use influence to map out the "real" organizational chart, as we showed when we installed sociometer software on the cell phones of ninety-four people in our laboratory.[14]

The sociometer data showed that people in the same group were more likely to coordinate their pattern of communication with others, and this mutual influence allowed us to identify teammates as well as predict one person's pattern of communication from that of their teammates. In contrast, simple measures like the time spent near each other or the number of meetings attended together gave no clue about group membership or organizational structure. This was because the groups usually had only one group meeting per week, and people's offices were freely mixed in with offices assigned to other groups.

In addition to identifying team members, you could identify the leaders of the teams. Whereas the communication patterns of the people in a team are predictable from other team members, the same was not true of the leader. The leader's pattern was *not* predictable from those of the team members. The communication pattern of the team, however, *could* be predicted from that of the leader. What we found was that the leader's pattern of communication drives the pattern of the team, just as the signaling associated with leading drives the pattern of conversational turn taking.

ELECTRONIC CIRCUITS

How does network intelligence—social signals, influence on social networks, idea markets, and so forth—translate to modern organizations, where electronic communications play an increasingly important role? To explore the relationship between the performance of an organization and its communication network, we can look again at our data from a German bank's marketing division. For this study, we asked the twenty-two employees to wear sociometers for an entire month and also recorded the email traffic between each employee.

This marketing division is a fairly traditional frontline business unit. It has regularly reviewed sales goals, and its twenty-two employees are organized into four groups with two layers of management. Like most real organizations, this marketing division is not housed in one office space. It is instead distributed around two floors of a large building, so that email became a critical part of its communications network.

When we compared email and face-to-face communication, we found that most people traded off face-to-face communication and email, choosing to use one communication channel or the other but not both.[15] The exception is when people spent a lot of time face-to-face working in close physical proximity. In this case, the number of emails increased along with the number of face-to-face encounters. It appears that when people work together, they begin to use email to supplement face-to-face conversation, rather like kids passing notes in a school class.

In this experiment we also measured people's judgments of productivity, job satisfaction, and the quality of group interaction. At the end of each day, each employee was asked to respond to an online survey that included the following questions: What was your level of job satisfaction today? What was the quality of your group interaction today? When we compared the results of these survey questions to the communication network, neither the network of email nor face-to-face communication was predictive of satisfaction or the quality of interaction. What we found was that job satisfaction and the group interaction quality were strongly dependent on the combination of face-to-face and email communication, or what we call "total communication."[16] While people liked to have more face-to-face communication with other people, both their job satisfaction and impression of group interaction quality were hurt by increasing the amount of total communication above a certain threshold.

Communication overload is not a big surprise, but what is surprising is that we couldn't see it without adding the sociometer data to the email data. The electronic circuits by themselves did not signal when people were overloaded.

We also found that people who were more central in the total communication network had worse impressions of the group interaction quality. So just as with the problem of detecting communication overload, we needed both the sociometer data and the electronic traffic to measure how well management was doing. This fits with what we saw when we examined our MIT laboratory with phone-based sociometers. The groups with the most centralized and stable communication networks felt the least job satisfaction and had the lowest group productivity.[17]

DISTRIBUTED CIRCUITS

Insights from these experiments offer some hope for teams that are distributed around the globe. It is widely thought that there are two critical problems for groups that primarily use electronic communications rather than face-to-face meetings.[18] The first is that such groups seem to lack the ability to harvest information that is distributed across the team rather than concentrated entirely in one or another team member. The second problem is that members of distance teams often experience a lack of both social integration and connection to the decision-making process.

Both of these problems may stem from a reliance on the centralized, language-based communications tools that are in use now. In today's systems, signaling between people is frequently minimized, and is usually confined to one person signaling at a time. But because social signaling is inherently a two-way process, memos and email simply don't work the same way that face-to-face communications work. When you send an email or issue a memo, the receiver is more likely to feel isolated from the decision making because they are missing the two-way engagement of social signaling.[19] They want to have their reaction carried back to the issuer; face-to-face communication accomplishes this because it is two-way, changing both the messenger as well as the receiver.

As a result of an overreliance on these language-based communication tools, the sort of dense network of social circuits needed to both support an idea market and enable people to read the group's network intelligence simply doesn't exist. These same limitations mean that people can't participate in the group's social circuitry, and as a result they feel that they have little influence on the group decision process.

One approach to curing these ills is to provide continuous signaling channels between all the participants, just as happens in face-to-face groups. Today there are many research laboratories exploring this possibility, using everything from high-end computer graphics avatars to low-end animated computer sprites. Only time will tell which, if any, of these approaches will be successful.

NEXT STEPS

Our sociometer data show us that modern organizations aren't really so different from early humans or even social animals such as bees. Honest signals are used to communicate, control the discovery and integration of information, and make decisions. The critical role that honest social signals play in almost every human interaction means that successful organizations should leverage these natural patterns of human social circuitry rather than trying to fight or ignore them.

We are just now beginning to understand how our ancient patterns of organization and communication translate to electronic media and distributed teams by using the sociometer to examine the behavior of entire organizations. We have seen that by combining the sociometer sensing of human interactions with the measurement of email, we can detect communication overloads and predict group interaction quality. As a consequence, we expect that our new abilities to sense organizational function will allow us to engineer better workplaces.

We have already made a start on this sort of organizational engineering with our Sensible Organizations program, the goal of which is to uncover the tacit patterns of behavior that lie behind the success of one firm and the failure of another.[20] For instance, by giving wirelessly connected sociometer badges to every person within the organization, Sensible Organizations technology allows people to monitor the flow of information within their group so that they can identify information bottlenecks and overloads.

The sociometer has given us a different view of human society— one that owes more to our ancient capacity for honest signaling than to our conscious mind, and one in which signaling within our social networks is seen as more powerful than logic or reason. In the next chapter, I will explore where this new sense of humanity might lead us.

7

SENSIBLE SOCIETIES

The next care to be taken, in respect of the Senses, is a supplying of their infirmities with Instruments, and as it were, the adding of artificial Organs to the natural . . . and as Glasses have highly promoted our seeing, so 'tis not improbable, but that there may be found many mechanical inventions to improve our other senses of hearing, smelling, tasting, and touching.

Robert Hooke, Preface to *Micrographia*, 1664

We can well imagine that other seventeenth-century scientists were skeptical about Hooke's vision of the future, but his predictions have been surprisingly accurate. His forecasts, however, overlooked a crucial sense: our social sense. Today, the sociometer and instruments like it enable a magnification of our social sense. Through these new instruments, we have the ability to look past our cultural and psychological biases and presuppositions to see ourselves from a new perspective. What difference might this new view of human behavior make?

New types of measurement instruments bring new data, which in turn lead to a new understanding of our world. To better appreciate the impact that a new type of measurement instrument can have, consider the humble optical lens of Hooke's era. This measurement technology became widely accessible in the early 1600s, and by the middle of that century this simple invention had already overthrown our concept of humanity's place in the world. Based on his telescope observations, Galileo Galilei's book *Sidereus Nuncius* (*Starry Messenger*) showed that the earth was not the center of the entire universe; if the earth was not the center, then perhaps humanity was not the crown of creation.

By the last half of the 1600s, when Hooke wrote about the wonders of the microscope, he was part of a full-fledged revolution created by the ability of the optical lens to enhance human vision. Hooke used optical lenses to look at microscopic life, and observed that humans were composed of small living cells, and that these same sorts of single-celled life-forms crawled on our skins and swam in our guts. He demonstrated that humans are not pristine creatures but instead are embedded in a swarm of microscopic life-forms, and our bodies are composed from these same tiny bits of life. Humanity no longer stood apart from the rest of creation.

The optical lens also allowed us to create accurate maps and was central to some of the greatest success stories in physics. Mapping and physics introduced the idea that our surrounding physical environment could be accurately measured and scientifically modified to achieve human goals. As with the microscope and telescope, these achievements were important in changing our idea about humanity's place in the world. Humans were now seen as masters of creation, no longer by divine right, but rather by the work of our own minds and hands.

The sociometer and instruments like it that allow for the continuous, quantitative measurement of human behavior will undoubtedly change our self-concept and worldview—but how? The impact of these new tools will likely happen in much the same manner as with previous measurement tools: by refining our sense of who we are, changing how we see others, and allowing us to better engineer our (social) environment. This final chapter will explore these themes and speculate about the changes that a new network science might bring.

SOCIAL FABRIC

Ever since Enlightenment philosophers overturned the belief that mysticism and revelation were the primary sources of knowledge and wisdom, a fundamental assumption has been that the rational, conscious, individual mind is the font of human intelligence.[1] We think of ourselves as independent, self-aware individuals, making decisions that shape our lives and carve out our place in the world. As a consequence of this viewpoint, our picture of society tends to be one of consciously interacting individuals, learning from each other by argument or example, and building organizations by using each other as convenient repositories of knowledge.[2]

The sociometer, though, reveals that there is more going on than just individuals engaging in conscious interaction. It shows us that our minds are also substantially *governed* by the unconscious signaling within the social fabric that surrounds us. Across a broad range of studies, human honest signals play an unexpectedly central role

in the decision making of individuals, groups, and even entire organizations. This mixture of unconscious signaling and conscious
interaction may explain why psychology studies repeatedly find that
our opinions are surprisingly predictable from our associates' opinions, even when they fly in the face of strong counterfactual evidence
or strongly held beliefs.[3] As a consequence, important parts of our
intelligence exist as *network properties*, not individual properties, and
important parts of our personal cognitive processes are *guided* by the
network via unconscious and automatic processes such as signaling
and imitation. Human intelligence is in *both* the individual and the
social network. We do not yet know which parts of our culture and
intelligence are due to network effects, and which are due to our
individual capabilities. Daniel Brown, for instance, has compiled a
list of almost four hundred traits shared by all known human cultures.[4] Which of these "universals" are due to the dynamics of our
unconscious interactions? Which stem primarily from our individual limitations or special talents? Until we have more thoroughly
sorted out the individual and network effects, it will be hard to
design better schools or companies.

What is clear is that social measurement tools such as the sociometer will change our concept of individual intelligence and our relationship with society. Just as the lens removed us from the center of
creation, we will come to realize that we bear little resemblance to
the idealized, rational beings imagined by Enlightenment philosophers. The idea that our conscious, individual thinking is the key
determining factor of our behavior may come to be seen as foolish
a vanity as our earlier idea that we were the center of the universe.

How will this awareness of the social fabric of human behavior
impact people's lives? Once you know that your decisions are

affected by the push and pull of those around you, how will we organize ourselves differently? To answer these questions, we will need to consider the functionality that drove the evolution of our unconscious social behaviors. In other words, we need to understand more clearly how our social fabric contributes to our individual and group intelligence.

NETWORK INTELLIGENCE

The idea that the patterns of unconscious social circuitry within groups can form a sort of decision-making machine is perhaps the first step toward explaining the adaptive utility of our unconscious social behaviors. In our experiments, it appears that our social signaling machine draws out proposals from individuals and processes them until one is selected as the group's decision. Rather than decision making based on syllogism, logic, and argument, this sort of group decision making is based on market principles, and uses social signaling to select actions that the group believes will minimize risk and maximize reward. And as we saw in chapter 5, this type of network intelligence can be more accurate than even the best individual intelligences.

This viewpoint of network intelligence runs counter to the intellectual tradition that views human intelligence as a property of the individual alone. But network intelligence is a good description for many examples of decision making ranging from apes and other animals to the interaction between signaling and decision making seen in modern business meetings.[5] Data from the sociometer show unsuspected parallels between our unconscious social fabric and the adaptive intelligences developed by other distributed biological systems. Just as the lens demonstrated our relationship to other life-forms, we will be able to use these new tools to achieve a better understanding of the evolution of intelligence in networks. Today our society is organized around conscious decision making. But a better understanding of how the structure of our social network and the character of our social signaling enable adaptive group intelligence will allow us to improve our decision-making abilities. We must ask how we can shift away from the rational actor approach to managing our society and instead focus more on shaping our social networks.

This change in perspective could have significant practical ramifications. Consider the management of companies, government agencies, and other similar organizations. A first step toward incorporating the network intelligence perspective would be to replace the static org chart with the idea of a network organization that varies over time, changing to suit the information-processing requirements of the task.[6] Organizations might also pay attention to maximizing everyone's ability to read the network of social interactions, so that the participants could more effectively integrate information and thus harvest their organizations' tacit knowledge.

Similar changes might apply to the organization of childhood learning. Rather than a primary focus on teaching individual cognitive skills, one might instead emphasize network interactions and seek to leverage group dynamics. At least some influential thinkers have argued that this sort of transformation of our schools is long overdue.[7]

This first step—to move from seeing human groups as a collection of individual intelligences bound together by language to viewing them as a network intelligence bound together by ancient signaling mechanisms—is essential. For only by taking this initial step can we begin to better channel and leverage our human network intelligence, using it to engineer our organizations as well as improve information aggregation and decision making, to change the management of organizations, political governance, education, and even the practice of science.

SOCIAL PHYSICS

The ability to continuously and universally measure human behavior will provide us with the ability to engineer our lives to an extent never before imagined. The hope is that with this combination of sociometer-style sensing and computational models of behavior, we can produce a sensible society—one that more closely matches our ideals and aspirations.

At present, we manage organizations by trying to influence conscious processes and explicit knowledge. Yet the sociometer data show that unconscious processes and tacit knowledge are potentially even more important in determining the behavior of organizations. To build really successful organizations, we must begin to account for the effects of social circuitry along with the more familiar types of conscious, language-based interaction.

To further these organizational engineering goals, we are using our Sensible Organizations technology to allow people to monitor the flow of information within their group, thereby transforming unconscious and tacit knowledge into open, conscious information.[8] Using this technology, we can know ourselves better and engineer our organizations to be places that better suit our human selves. We may even be able to "tune" our social networks to promote greater trust, openness, and enthusiasm.

Beyond organizational engineering is the possibility of building physicslike models of human behavior, coined "social physics" by Mark Buchanan, a former editor of *Nature*.[9] A social physics would allow us to discover fundamental laws that govern all human organizations. If human behavior were largely governed by logical argument and conscious decision, we could not build such models because there would be no fixed laws beyond those that stem directly from the definition of rationality. The sociometer data, however, reveal a different side of humanity—one in which humans react to each other in a regular and predictable manner.

As a proof in principle, we used this physicslike approach to model the patterns within 330,000 hours of sociometer data from ninety-four people at MIT. We discovered that a social physics model could predict people's day-to-day and person-to-person communication with more than 95 percent accuracy and surprisingly few parameters.[10] Moreover, the same model could accurately predict job satisfaction and even creative productivity.[11]

This predictability is exactly what opens up the possibility of creating a social physics. The predictive power of the social signals measured by the sociometer is surprisingly powerful and uniform across different situations. Thus, we can use these signals to predict behaviors with very good accuracy, even without adjusting for personal characteristics or the history of previous interactions. By combining these individual predictions across people and situations, we may be able to make accurate predictions about the behavior of even the largest human organizations.

Today we can sense the physical environment in great detail, but can measure only certain average properties of human behavior—for example, the amount of traffic on a highway or the number of phone calls made. In the future, we will have the capacity to sense the human environment as accurately as the physical environment. This will give us microscopic knowledge of organizations and even entire societies, and allow us to build physicslike models of the behavior of human populations.

The combination of these evolving sensory systems with computational models of social interaction will soon lead to the ability to model, predict, and influence the behavior of both individuals and whole societies. The hope is that by combining sensor networks and computational models of behavior, we can produce a sensible society—one that can address global problems where the cooperation of virtually everyone is required, such as global warming, SARS and infectious disease, strife due to cultural collisions, and the livability of our cities.

CONCLUSION

Revolutionary new measurement tools such as the sociometer are providing us with a God's eye view of ourselves. For the first time, we can precisely map the behavior of large numbers of people as they go about their daily lives. Through many different studies in various settings, we found that a surprising amount of human behavior can be reliably predicted from these biologically based honest signals. By measuring and modeling these social signals, we have argued that our patterns of communication and the shapes of our social networks are tied to the characteristics of this unconscious communication channel.

Stepping back to view the broad picture revealed by an analysis of these human honest signals, we have been able to understand why our unconscious social behavior is adaptive, and how it could have been adaptive even before the development of sophisticated language abilities. Our proposal is that the patterns of social signaling that we measure are in fact quite sophisticated systems for information discovery, integration, and decision making. Taken together, these systems can create a network intelligence that is broadly superior to individual human intelligence.

The sociometer has given us a new, powerful way to understand and manage human groups, corporations, and entire societies. As this new account of human social behavior becomes refined by the use of more sophisticated statistical models and sensor capabilities, we could well see the creation of a quantitative, predictive science of human organizations and human society. Just as we are beginning to be able to engineer our genes, we are also beginning to be able to engineer our society, producing "designer societies" that work dramatically better than today's natural ones. At the same time, these new tools have the potential to make George Orwell's vision of an all-controlling state into a reality. What we do with this new power may turn out to be either our salvation or destruction.

EPILOGUE: TECHNOLOGY AND SOCIETY

Wouldn't it be wonderful if human organizations just worked? Imagine a world in which it is normal to openly speak your concerns, to have a fair and honest group discussion, and in which people are enthusiastic about carrying through group decisions in a transparent and comprehensive way. Given the variety and frequency of jokes about bad meetings, and indeed about failed communication in general, such meetings and enthusiasm seem destined to remain wishful thinking.

Although developers of communication-support tools have certainly tried to create products that support group thinking, they usually do so without adequately accounting for the social context, so that all too often these systems are jarring and even downright rude. In fact, most people would agree that today's communication technology seems to be at war with human society.

One consequence of our society's infatuation with the concept of the rational human is that our technology treats people like cogs in an information-processing machine. The result is that current communications technology doesn't feel good. Buzzing pagers, ringing cell phones, and barrages of emails are leashes that keep people tethered to their job, and people worry that we are being drawn into some sort of electronic hell. Technologists have responded with interfaces that pretend to have feelings or call us by name, filters that attempt to shield us from the digital onslaught, and smart devices that organize our lives by gossiping behind our backs. But the result usually feels like it was designed to keep us isolated, wandering like a clueless extra in a cold virtual world.

These well-meaning solutions ultimately fail because they ignore the core problem: computers are socially ignorant. Technology must account for this by recognizing that communication is always socially situated, and that discussions are not just words but also part of a larger social dialogue. Successful human communicators universally recognize that communication is part of an evolving social process, and use this fact to their advantage. Digital communications can begin to do the same by trying to quantify the social context and then understanding how this context can be used to select successful interaction behaviors.

Our new capability for the measurement of social context permits the communications system to support social and organizational roles instead of viewing the individual as an isolated entity.[1] Example applications include automatically patching people into socially important conversations, instigating conversations among people in order to build a more solid social network, and reinforcing family ties. The implications of a system that can measure the social context are particularly important in a mobile, geographically dispersed society.

Propagating the social context could transform distance learning, for instance, letting users become better integrated into ongoing projects and discussions, and thus improve social interaction, teamwork, and social networking. Teleconferencing might become more reflective of actual human contact, since the participants can now quantify the communication's value. Automatic help desks might be able to abandon their robotic, information-only delivery or inappropriately cheerful replies.

These changes are just beginning, however. Ten years ago, half of humanity had never made a phone call and only 20 percent had regular access to communications. Today 70 percent of humanity can place a telephone call, or more likely, send an SMS message to the secretary general of the United Nations or most anyone else. Because remanufactured cell phones cost $10 in the developing world and incoming messages are free, almost every stratum of society is now connected.

For the first time, the majority of humanity is connected and has a voice. The most important changes will come, though, because these same cell phones are also sociometers. Their sociometer functionality is mostly latent at this point, but already these devices can determine their location, record who else is nearby, and measure the social signals in their owner's voice.

The sociometer functionality of cell phone networks is what governments such as India are using to track terrorists, and they claim that the vast majority of captured terrorists have been identified through cell phone transactions. The sociometer-style ability of cell phone networks to identify unusual patterns of movement and communication are also how public health officials and disaster relief teams are scanning for outbreaks of diseases like SARS and emergencies such as tidal waves. On a more individual level, cities are now investigating the use of cell phone networks to control automobile traffic, and doctors are exploring how to use changes in patients' patterns of voice and movement to help in the early identification of disease.

It seems that the human race suddenly has the beginnings of a working nervous system.[2] Like some world-spanning living organism, public health systems, automobile traffic, and emergency and security networks are all becoming intelligent, reactive systems with sociometer-style sensors serving as their eyes and ears. The evolution of this nervous system will continue at a quickening speed because of Moore's law and basic economics. The networks will be come faster, the devices will have more sensors, and the techniques for modeling human behavior will become more accurate and detailed. The combination of this evolving nervous system with models of social physics will soon lead to the ability to engineer our societies and entire culture.

For society, the hope is that we can use this new digital nervous system to address global problems where the cooperation of virtually everyone is required. For individuals, the attraction is the possibility of a world where everything is arranged for your convenience—the bus appears just when you need it, your health checkup is magically scheduled just as you begin to get sick, and airport security is a thing of the past. The trade-offs, however, of privacy versus convenience, individual freedom versus societal benefit, and our sense of individuality versus group identity may be greater than any humanity has faced before. We are living in interesting times indeed.

APPENDIX A: SOCIAL SCIENCE BACKGROUND

Decades of research in social psychology illustrate the surprising ability of humans to read each other. From contexts as diverse as evaluating classroom teachers, selecting job applicants, or predicting the outcomes of court cases, human judgments made on the basis of just a thin slice of observational data can be highly predictive of later behavior.

The term thin slice comes from a frequently cited article by Nalini Ambady and Robert Rosenthal, in which subjects evaluated thirty-second silent video clips of instructors teaching a class.[1] Subsequent analysis found that these brief evaluations predicted the instructors' end-of-semester student ratings. Their work built on earlier research that found a similar predictive power in job interviews,[2] where the first impressions were critical for the eventual hiring decision.[3]

Thin slices of behavioral data have been shown to predict a broad range of consequences, including therapist competency ratings,[4] the personalities of strangers,[5] and even courtroom judges' expectations for criminal trial outcomes.[6] One of the most impressive examples of thin slices predicting important, long-term consequences is the marital research conducted by John Gottman and his colleagues.[7] Sybil Carrère and Gottman were able to predict marital outcomes over a six-year period based on human microcoding of just the first three minutes of a marital conflict.[8]

Across a wide range of studies, Ambady and Rosenthal[9] found that observations lasting up to five minutes had an average correlation of $r = .39$ with subsequent behavior, which corresponds to 70 percent accuracy at predicting outcomes (for a definition of the correlation r and accuracy, see the "Methods for the Experiments" section below).[10] It is astounding that the observation of such a thin slice of behavior can predict crucial behavioral outcomes such as professional competence, criminal conviction, and divorce, when the predicted outcome is sometimes months or years in the future. What is it that people are seeing in these thin slices of behavior?

The key lies in understanding the complete picture of social signaling. Animals communicate and negotiate their position within a social hierarchy in many ways, including dominance displays, relative positioning, and access to resources. Humans add a wide variety of cultural mechanisms to that repertoire such as clothing, seating arrangements, and name-dropping.[11] Most of these culture-specific social communications are conscious and easily manipulated.

In many situations, however, other nonlinguistic—and often unconscious—social signals (e.g., body language, facial expressions, and tone of voice) are as significant as conscious linguistic content in predicting behavioral outcomes.[12] Such unconscious behaviors may have originally evolved as grooming, dominance, and similar social signals, but continue to exist today as a complement to human language.[13]

While the human ability to judge outcomes from thin slices of behavior has been well documented, there is little understanding about which signals people are using to make these judgments. In part this is because the signals are unconscious and therefore their nature is not obvious. But an even larger obstacle is that it requires sophisticated signal processing to build the proper measurement tools. This unusual combination of psychology and signal-processing expertise is what has allowed our research group to build tools such as the sociometer, which allow for the quantitative, continuous measurement of human social signaling.

MEASURING SOCIAL SIGNALS: THE SOCIOMETER

Historically, our understanding of social interaction has been limited to relatively sparse observations of small groups due to the constraints of the measurement tools available. Recent advances in sensor networks and mobile computing, though, have greatly improved our measurement capabilities. As a result, we can now build devices that can accurately and continuously track the behavior of hundreds or even thousands of humans at a time, recording even the finest scale behaviors with high accuracy.

My students and I have built several generations of what we call sociometers, using cell phones and electronic badges with integrated sensors. With a wide range of collaborators, we have been able to observe hundreds of people for periods of up to a year, in the process amassing hundreds of thousands of hours of data.

The first sociometer, which I created with Tanzeem Choudhury along with design help from Brian Clarkson, was able to measure face-to-face interactions between people using an infrared transceiver (to detect when people were facing each other), a microphone (to collect sound), and a two-axis accelerometer (to measure body motion).[14] This badge was used to extract social interactions from sensory data, and then model the structure and dynamics of social networks. Following the success of this first sociometer, several generations of badgelike sociometers have been created, each with improved capabilities and hardware design.[15]

The current sociometer, created by Daniel Olguin and his colleagues, is lightweight and has a small badgelike form factor in order to be comfortable to wear for long periods of time.[16] It also has a long battery life so that it doesn't need to be charged every day. To achieve this, the badge is designed for low power wake-up directly from sensor stimuli. The main measurement features offered by the current sociometer are:

- Capturing face-to-face interactions using an infrared sensor to determine how much time users spend talking face-to-face
- Performing speech feature analysis to measure nonlinguistic social signals and identify the social context
- Recognizing common daily human activities by measuring body movement
- Performing indoor tracking and user localization
- Communicating with cell phones and computers in order to send and receive information from different users as well as process data
- Measuring the physical proximity to other people

QUANTIFYING SOCIAL SIGNALS

The computer and signal-processing research communities have studied human communication at many timescales—for example, phonemes, words, phrases, and dialogues—and both semantic and prosodic structures have been analyzed. Yet the sort of longer-term, multiutterance structure associated with the signaling of social attitude (e.g., interested, attracted, confrontational, friendly, etc.) has received little attention.

On the basis of a broad reading of the voice analysis, animal communication, and social science literature, we developed an approach to quantify human honest signals. Our analyses yielded texturelike measures for four types of social signaling, which were designated as activity level, influence, consistency, and mimicry.[17]

By using these measurements to quantify the honest signaling in face-to-face discussions, we can anticipate outcomes by learning the relationship between signaling and behavior. Because studies of human expression have shown high correlations between measures of vocal prosody, facial gesture, and hand gesture, our measures of signaling were designed to be able take advantage of either gesturing or prosody. This redundancy is attributed to what is known as the *excitatory hypothesis*: a single excitatory impulse will show *parallel* changes in the modalities of voice prosody, face gesture, and body gesture.[18]

ACTIVITY Our simplest measure is activity, which we usually quantify by measuring the amount of time a person is active. In many of our experiments this is simply the fraction of time a person is speaking. Similarly, for hand, face, and body gesture we can measure the fraction of time people are moving around. This movement measure typically has a threshold so that only relatively large gestures get counted, in order to avoid being confused by simple posture changes.

Previous research shows that the percentage of speaking time is correlated with interest level and extraversion. Likewise, a recent meta-analysis found a high correlation between speaking time and individual dominance.[19] Indeed, in studies involving competitive settings similar to a negotiation, speaking time is positively correlated with dominance over the outcome.[20]

INFLUENCE Influence is measured by the amount of control that one person has on the other's behavior. When two people are engaged in conversation their individual turn-taking patterns influence one another, and the resulting pattern of turn taking can be modeled as a Markov process.[21] By quantifying the conditional probability of person A's current state (speaking versus not speaking) given person B's previous state, we obtain a measure of person B's influence over the turn-taking behavior. If two individuals are practically talking over one another, then both may have high influence scores, whereas long, irregular pauses between speakers would lead to low influence scores. One-sided influence typically occurs when one person is energetically questioning another, and the other begins speaking only after the questioner ceases talking.

Recent evidence from research on competitive tasks suggests that both power and status are mediated by a partner's attention, and influence can be used as a measure of the attention paid by one participant to another. In one of the first studies to formalize this measure of attention, Joseph Jaffe and his colleagues found that the timing of vocalizations between four-month-old infants and their caregivers was predictive of infants' cognitive and social development as measured at twelve months.[22]

CONSISTENCY   Consistency is measured by the amount of *variation* in speech prosody or gesture—for example, the variation in pitch, volume, and rhythm while speaking, or the variation in speed, size, or acceleration while gesturing.[23] If a person starts out speaking calmly and evenly, for instance, and then becomes progressively more excited, they are likely to have a low consistency score (or equivalently, a high variability score).

The importance of consistency and variation in speech prosody as a communication signal has a long history in child development research. For instance, many researchers have argued that mothers' use of exaggerated pitch peaks to mark focused words helps infants to learn to speak.[24] Words with consistent prosody are "normal," while words with high variability are "special" and the infant should pay special attention to them.

The lack of consistency in speech prosody (i.e., high variability) is often a sign of emotionality.[25] It is also an indication of cognitive load. In fact, one of the most common measures of cognitive load is simply the amount of the irregularity and delay present in a conversational turn-taking task.[26]

MIMICRY   When one person mimics or mirrors the behavior of another, this frequently signals empathy, and has been shown to positively influence the smoothness of an interaction as well as mutual liking.[27] The unconscious mimicry of others' behaviors (e.g., body movements, facial expressions, or speech) seems to serve an adaptive social function.[28] For example, waitresses who mimic the speech style of their customers receive more tips than those who do not.[29]

Measuring mimicry is hard, because there are so many aspects of our behavior that can be mimicked. Fortunately, there seems to be a simple "proxy" measurement for the full range of mimicry: the short back-and-forth exchanges that are sprinkled throughout typical conversations. These include reciprocated head nods, back-and-forth exchanges of single words (e.g., "OK?" "OK!" "Done?" "Yup"), and copied posture changes, all of which can be measured by our current sociometer. We therefore treat the occurrence of these short back-and-forth exchanges (e.g., reciprocated short utterances) as a proxy for overall mimicry.

A NEW INTERPRETATION FRAMEWORK FOR SOCIAL INTERACTION

Social interaction has traditionally been addressed within two different frameworks. One framework comes from cognitive psychology and focuses largely on emotion. The key idea is that people perceive others' emotions through stereotyped displays of facial expression, tone of voice, and so forth. The simplicity and perceptual grounding of this theory has recently given rise to considerable interest in the scientific and engineering literature.[30] In practice, however, it has been difficult to measure these displays and even more difficult to use them to build practical applications such as user support systems. This is partly because adults are skilled at hiding emotions, partly because seemingly identical behaviors have different emotional roots, and partly because it has proven extremely difficult to build tools that can reliably measure these subtle movements.

The second framework for understanding social interaction comes from linguistics. It approaches social interaction from the viewpoint of dialogue understanding, so that vocal prosody and gesture are treated as annotations of linguistic information rather than as first-class communication signals. As an example, prosody (variations in the pitch and amplitude of the speaker's voice) and gesture (e.g., pointing or looking at something) could be used to guide attention and signal irony.[31] In practice, this framework has proven useful for computer graphics and language production systems, but has been difficult to apply to dialogue interpretation, perception, and unconscious behaviors generally. It has thus been difficult to use this approach in practical applications such as travel reservations or banking systems.

This book develops an alternative, third interpretation framework—honest signaling—in which speaker *attitude* or *intention* is conveyed through unconscious behavior, such as changes in the amplitude and frequency of prosodic and gestural activities. This framework is based on the literature of animal communication[32] and social psychology,[33] and is different from the linguistic framework in that it centers on nonlinguistic, unconscious signals about the social situation.

Similarly, it differs from the affect interpretation framework in that it concerns social relations rather than speaker emotion. That is, honest signals communicate about the *relationship* between people rather than about the content of the dialogue. Honest signaling is what you perceive, for example, when observing a conversation in an unfamiliar language and yet find that you can still "see" someone taking charge of a conversation, or establishing a friendly interaction.[34]

The honest signaling framework developed in this book differs in yet another significant way: its measurements happen over longer time frames than typical linguistic phenomena or emotional displays, treating gestures more like a motion texture than individual actions. As a result, these honest signals constitute an independent channel of communication.

METHODS FOR THE EXPERIMENTS

Most psychology experiments have a similar design: two groups, a control group and a test group, are used to test a single, fixed hypothesis. The fields of machine learning, signal processing, and artificial intelligence typically conduct experiments differently: performance and contextual data are collected from subjects doing a naturalistic task, with the natural variations between people playing the roles of test and control groups. In this way, a rule that relates contextual variables (like social signaling measures) to performance data (like salary) can be deduced.

To make sure that the results are not due to some accidental feature of the data, the data are divided in various ways to test how representative each subgroup is of all the others. This process is called cross-validation. In other words, if the same relationship is found in each subgroup, then you can expect that data from future groups will be similar, and the rule that relates contextual variables to outcomes will hold generally.

This is the typical methodology for the experiments described in this book. The subjects performed a task while we used sociometers to measure social signals (e.g., usually measures of vocal activity, influence, consistency, and mimicry). We then compared the signaling to the outcome of the task—for example: How big a raise did they get? Did they exchange phone numbers?

To determine which social signals are related to the behavior outcome, we used linear regression modeling. Regression is a mathematical method of fitting a line to data; the position and angle (slope) of this line determines how much an increase in the social signal increases the likelihood of the behavior.

Because there are several social signals, we used a slightly more complex fitting method called stepwise linear regression. This lets us discover the *combinations* of social signals that when taken together, predict the maximum amount of variance in behavioral outcomes. In all of these stepwise regressions, we added signals to the regression if their p value (see below) was less than 0.05, and removed them if their p value was greater than 0.10.

Typically, we would run this stepwise regression forward and backward: starting with all the signals, and then again starting with none of the signals. If the same combination of signals is selected both times, then we can be confident that these are really the "right" signals to predict the behavior. We would then use cross-validation to make sure that the rule relating signals to outcomes was not an accidental result and would generalize to new data.

We assessed the strength of the model produced by this regression by reporting standard statistics:

r: The *correlation coefficient*, ranging from −1 to 1, measures the strength of a linear relationship. Values close to 1 indicate a strong positive relationship, values close to −1 indicate a strong negative relationship, and values near 0 indicate a weak (linear) relationship.

r^2: The square of the correlation coefficient, which is a measure of what percentage of the total amount of variation has been accounted for by the mathematical model.

p: The p value is the probability that we could observe this value of r by chance, assuming that there were no true underlying relationship. Smaller p values indicate more statistically significant findings.

DECISION ACCURACY   This number measures the strength of a model attempting to separate sample data into two mutually exclusive, collectively exhaustive classes (e.g., success *versus* failure). Reported as a percentage, it tells us what proportion of the observations was correctly classified. The incorrect classifications are then divided into *false positives* (with failure classified as success) and *false negatives* (with success classified as failure). We usually try to make these two types of errors equally probable.

When describing the strength of the results, we follow the standard guidelines used in social science: a "medium effect size" is when $r \approx 0.30$ (so that r^2, the variance accounted for, is about 0.1), a "large effect size" is when $r \approx 0.50$ (so that r^2, the variance accounted for, is about 0.25), and a "very large effect size" is when $r \approx 0.65$ (so that r^2, the variance accounted for, is about 0.4). Analogously, we will describe 70 percent decision accuracy as "fairly accurate" (this is the typical accuracy for human thin-slicing decisions), 80 percent decision accuracy as "good accuracy," and 90 percent decision accuracy as "very accurate."

In terms of statistical significance, we generally use $p < 0.01$, which is a relatively strict cutoff for accepting a relationship.

SUMMARY

Social science has firmly established that people can accurately read each other in thirty-second thin slices of observation, assessing social attitudes such as attention, interest, empathy, determination, and openness. How people do this has not been known, although there are many clues scattered across the scientific literature.

Using these clues about "people reading," we have developed computer signal-processing tools for measuring four types of unconscious behaviors that function as honest signals of the social relations. We have packaged our computer tools into a badgelike device called a sociometer, which has given us the ability for simultaneous, continuous, real-time assessment of social interaction among hundreds of people.

Using our sociometers, we have conducted many experiments relating human signaling and patterns of interaction to behavioral outcomes. We have found that we can use the sociometer measurements to accurately predict outcomes in situations such as negotiations, dating, selling, bluffing, and other critical human activities. The following several appendixes describe our experiments and their results.

APPENDIX B: SUCCESS

We spend much of our time interacting and negotiating with other people to get the resources and opportunities that interest us. Unlike a formal negotiation, this is a continuous process that includes many stages: detecting a flicker of interest in a potential customer or partner, proposing your idea, listening carefully to the response, and finally negotiating the details.

Honest signals play a central role in each step of this complex social process. In the experiments below, we have explored the crucial links formed by honest signals in situations ranging from salary negotiations and call center interactions to business plan pitches.

MEASURING INTEREST

The first step toward success is often detecting interest in potential customers or partners. In order to understand which social signals convey interest, Anmol Madan and I conducted a study[1] with twenty participants, ten males and ten females, paired up with a same-sex conversational partner. Each pair participated in ten successive short three-minute conversations on topics randomly selected from a "hot topics" list within a commercial news feed. The total duration of each session was approximately thirty minutes. Each conversational partner was wearing a sociometer, allowing us to unobtrusively measure their vocal social signaling. Finally, after each short conversation, subjects rated how interesting they found the conversation on a scale of 1 to 10, with 10 being the most interesting.

RESULTS For both men and women, the social signals extracted were significantly correlated with the self-reported interest labels. The activity and variable emphasis (low consistency) measures had a significant correlation with the interest ratings ($r = 0.6$, $p < 0.01$). The activity measure alone produced a correlation of $r = 0.50$, $p < 0.01$.

The overall distribution of interest ratings can be split into a two-class model: those labeled as high interest (all ratings 8 and above) and low interest (all ratings less than 8). Using the social signals of activity and consistency, we classified conversations into high- and low-interest groups with an accuracy of 75 percent.

DISCUSSION As expected, the activity measure was the strongest predictor of interest. Variable emphasis (low consistency), an honest signal of openness to information, was also significantly related to interest rating. Together, these two signals comprise the exploring display discussed in the main text—exactly what you would expect people to display when they were interested in a conversation topic.

ELEVATOR PITCHES

Having detected interest in a potential customer or partner, the next step is often to pitch an idea or a plan. To examine this step in working with others, I collected data with Will Stoltzman during sessions where MBA students from MIT's Sloan School of Management were practicing pitching business plans in preparation for a business plan contest.[2]

The students all had previous business experience, and the business plan contest involved rating by senior venture capital partners, with the best plans receiving seed funding. In each session, the participants gave a short, prepared pitch on their plan while wearing the sociometer. Most pitches were, of course, funding requests for new technology ventures. Each session consisted of roughly ten participants, and in total, we recorded and processed audio information from forty-two pitches (twenty males and twenty-two females) through the sociometers.

After each speaker presented a pitch, but before any group feedback, the listeners (who were also MBA students) filled out an anonymous survey and answered three questions (with words italicized as shown):

Question 1   How *persuasive* is the speaker, apart from the details of the pitch?

Question 2   How convincing is the *content* of the pitch, apart from the way in which the speaker delivered it (e.g., if you had *read* it)?

Question 3 How effective is the *presentation style,* apart from the details of the pitch and the way in which the speaker delivered it? (Presentation style addresses the number of "ums," the sentence structure, pacing, the flow of information, etc.)

Each question could be scored from 1 ("hardly") to 10 ("very"). The surveys were collected after each pitch, encouraging the participants to rate all the speakers independently, rather than comparatively within a session.

RESULTS The three survey questions (Q1, Q2, and Q3) were intentionally designed in order to isolate three different aspects of a pitch: persuasion, content, and style. Somewhat surprisingly, we found that these factors are highly intertwined. Taking the pair-wise correlations between the speakers' average scores on each of the three questions shows clear relationships:

$$r(Q1; Q2) = 0.83; \; r(Q1; Q3) = 0.94; \; r(Q2; Q3) = 0.77$$

Here all three *p* values are less than 0.01. The high correlations among these questions indicate that even experienced business-people are not good at distinguishing between content and style. Your ability to persuade a crowd may have as much to do with your presentation style as with your message.

The single feature we found to be most correlated with high marks in persuasiveness was activity with $r = 0.46, p = 0.003$—which in this single-speaker situation means that persuasive speakers talked faster than others. The consistency measure also showed a statistically significant trend ($r = 0.34, p = 0.03$). This indicates that persuasive speakers employ better-regulated emphasis. By combining these two explanatory variables, we achieved a correlation of $r = 0.6$, $p < 0.01$ between the social signals and the ratings of persuasiveness.

DISCUSSION These results indicate that the characteristics of what we have termed the *leading display*—signals of interest and certainty as shown through high activity and consistent emphasis—produce the highest-rated business pitches. This finding agrees with a study on charisma by Andrew Rosenberg and Julia Hirschberg, who found that higher activity levels (specifically, a faster speaking rate in terms of syllables per second) corresponded to a higher charisma rating.[3] In situations with question-and-answer periods, we would expect that high engagement (the only signal in the leading display that requires interaction) would also be an important predictor of success.

SUCCESSFUL SALES

Having detected interest and pitched your idea, the next step is to get the buyer or partner to agree—in other words, to "close the sale." Call centers are increasingly essential in closing sales, but unfortunately customer satisfaction with call center interactions is often quite low, and relatively little work has been done in suggesting what variables are related to caller satisfaction. This situation naturally suggests the question of how the signaling between call agents and customers affects call center success.

To test the role of social signals in call center interactions, Stoltzman and I worked with Vertex, one of the United Kingdom's largest providers of business process outsourcing—a collaboration arranged by Scotland's Highlands and Islands development authority and Strathclyde University.[4] In particular, we worked with their customer service branch in a call center serving Tesco PLC. Based in the United Kingdom, Tesco is one of the world's leading international retailers, with sales of £37.1 billion (approximately US$70 billion) in 2005.

We used the sociometer to collect speech features from customer service agents handling calls about a Tesco home product. All manner of calls relating to this product were processed, including sales, cancellations, questions, billing problems, complaints, and so on, and were thirty seconds or longer. Over a period of two days, we gathered information from seventy such calls, handled by eight different agents (two males and six females). Immediately after each call, the agent was asked to declare the call as "successful" or "unsuccessful." Of our seventy samples, thirty-nine were rated as successful, with the balance rated unsuccessful.

RESULTS   Considering just the agents' speech features, we found that variable emphasis (low consistency), low activity, and longer call times hold explanatory power in identifying successful sales calls ($r = 0.71$, $p < 0.01$).[5] Next, looking at the callers' speech features, we found that the features that correlate with a successful call (bearing in mind that success here is still defined from the agent's viewpoint) are variable emphasis (low consistency), high activity, and longer call times ($r = 0.6$, $p \ll 0.01$).[6] Finally, when we combined both the agents' and the callers' speech features, we achieved a correlation of $r = 0.76$, $p \ll 0.01$.

DISCUSSION   We found that success in a sales call is a predictable function of the social signaling. Analyzing audio streams from both the agent and the caller yields a prediction accuracy of 87 percent in classifying a call as successful or not. In cases where one or the other audio stream is not available (for technical reasons or privacy concerns), predictions made from just one of the participants are nearly as potent as those made from both streams because the agent and customer behaviors are complementary.

These findings offer a reasonable interpretation about what constitutes good customer service. First, the fact that longer call duration correlates with success shows that more interaction between the agent and the caller is fruitful. For the agent, variable emphasis seems to signal openness to comment or new information, and low activity (short speaking segments) left ample opportunities for the customer to speak. Simply put, successful calls tended to involve agents who display active listening, signaling that they are receptive to and interested in the caller.

SALARY NEGOTIATION

In complex situations, simply getting to "yes" isn't the end of the process. One must also negotiate the details—a step that is fraught with potential pitfalls. Most people have the intuition that negotiation is among the most rational forms of communication; this presents an interesting arena to probe whether social signals play a significant role.

To test this question, Jared Curhan and I examined the problem of negotiating a salary package with your boss.[7] We used the sociometer to collect social signals from forty-six gender-matched negotiation pairs (twenty-eight male and eighteen female pairs) who were asked to conduct a face-to-face negotiation as part of their class work. The negotiation involved a middle manager applying for a transfer to a vice president's division in their company, and required the negotiation of salary, vacation, company car, division, and health care benefits. These were summed into an overall objective score based on their market value. The subjects, who were first-year business students at MIT Sloan School of Management, were offered a real monetary incentive for maximizing their own individual outcome in the negotiation.

A total of fifty-four hours of data were collected, but we used only the first five minutes of the negotiation for analysis, taking a thin slice approach to predicting the final negotiation outcome. Subjective features were also analyzed, including answers to the following questions: What kind of impression do you think you made on your counterpart? To what extent did your counterpart deliberately let you get a better deal than they did? To what extent did you steer clear of disagreements?

RESULTS We found that the vice president's total score was strongly correlated with activity and influence, but also with the middle manager's activity and variability of emphasis. These signals predicted a total of 27 percent of the variance, with $r = 0.52$, $p < 0.01$. On the other hand, the middle manager's total score was strongly correlated with mimicry and consistency, but also with the vice president's variability in emphasis (low consistency). The regression predicted a total of 30 percent of the variance, with $r = 0.55$, $p < 0.01$.

These results treat the *pair* of people as the unit of analysis; we can also ask what aspects of *individual* signaling can lead to a better result.[8] To answer this question we used a much more sophisticated statistical analysis model (the Actor Partner Interdependence Model) to obtain actor and partner effects through hierarchical linear modeling. Including all four speech features (activity, influence, consistency, and mimicry), the model predicted a total of 30 percent of the variance in individual points (r^2 for middle managers = 0.36, r^2 for vice presidents = 0.23).[9]

In contrast to the unified analysis of the social signaling, when the roles are separated out, the significant features for the vice president were activity and consistency. Influence, which is a cooperative behavior, was separated out as a characteristic of the *pair* of people, not of the individual. For the middle manager, the significant features were consistency and mimicry, unchanged from the results of the pairwise analysis.

Of particular interest are the correlations with the subjective questions asked at the end of the negotiation, since subjective factors such as reputation and cooperation are important in situations where there are repeated negotiations between the same two people. We found that a subject's influence on their partner had a significant positive correlation with the subjective "impression I thought I made on my partner" rating ($r = 0.63$, $p < 0.01$), and with the "did your partner let you win" rating ($r = 0.65$, $p < 0.01$). The mimicry measure had a significant positive correlation with the extent to which participants said they were seeking to avoid disagreements ($r = 0.62$, $p < 0.01$).

DISCUSSION The social signaling occurring within the first five minutes of these negotiations was highly predictive of the final financial outcomes. Perhaps the most telling finding was that the signaling associated with success for the high-status parties was different from that associated with success for the low-status parties. In plain language, high-status negotiators need to display leading signals (activity, influence, and consistency) whereas low-status negotiators need to display teaming signals (influence, mimicry, and consistency).

SIGNALING AND SOCIAL ROLE   To understand in more detail how signaling and social roles work together, and how they change during a conversation, we also analyzed the social signaling in these fifty-four hours of negotiations on a minute-by-minute basis.[10] In particular, we examined these negotiations for patterns in the social signaling—that is, when one person answers another's signaling in a predictable manner.

What we found was that the roles and signaling of the two participants are strongly coupled, forming a continuous dance of signal and response. Often this dance was simply adopting the matching role; for instance, when one participant began to lead the conversational turn taking, the other participant almost always followed suit (90 percent of the time), resulting in a highly engaged, roughly equal conversation. When one participant displayed teaming behavior, the other would usually join in (74 percent of the time).

The results of this role taking, however, depended on the status of the participant. This is consistent with previous research that has found that dominant and submissive roles within pairs complement each other, and contribute to defining status and hierarchy within organizations.[11] For example, the leading role was, unsurprisingly, good for vice presidents but not for middle managers. Conversely, teaming behavior benefited middle managers but not vice presidents.

Responses to uncertainty or emotionality, as evidenced by variable emphasis (low consistency), also depend on the status. If the vice president showed variable emphasis, then the middle manager would usually become more active and only occasionally would respond with a display of variable emphasis. When the middle manager showed variable emphasis, the vice president would often also become more active, but was more than twice as likely to respond with matching variable emphasis. The conclusion is that the vice presidents were less reluctant than the middle managers to match displays of emotionality or uncertainty. It seems that rank apparently has its privileges, even though the data show that the vice presidents who responded with variable emphasis ended up with worse deals than those who kept a stiff upper lip.

These data clearly show that social signaling is dynamic; one person's signaling leads to responses that provoke further responses and so on, creating a sort of social dance of signal and response. Nor are these innately determined signals that provoke an automatic response; instead, the response depends on the participants' roles—the pattern of signal and response is different depending on whether the signal is from the boss or the new employee.

POKER FACES

Sometimes you have to fake it. And where better to study bluffing than in poker? Mike Sung and I monitored thirty-one tournaments, representing over four hundred hands of poker.[12] Every subject was paired up with another player to play real live-money games of no-limit Texas hold'em in heads-up style tournaments. Players' tournament games typically lasted between ten and thirty minutes.

As financial interest is instrumental in generating the stressful situations for this study, the players were asked to play in winner-takes-all tournaments with real money buy-ins. The subjects were paired with other players who shared similar financial risk thresholds (with a buy-in between five and twenty dollars per tournament). Each player's self-reported skill level and risk tolerance was also recorded in order to match the players as well as to provide additional baseline information. The study population was drawn from the MIT community who answered recruitment emails sent to the MIT poker mailing list. All the subjects were self-reported poker aficionados who played semiregularly, though the skill level ranged from beginners to players who play for profit in high-limit games.

In addition to sociometer analysis, the subjects were asked to fill out a form at the end of each hand indicating the player's mental state; this consisted of their self-reported interest, excitement, happiness, and stress levels rated on a scale of 1 to 10. The outcome data on whether the individual won or lost, whether they bluffed (small bluff, medium bluff, large bluff, or partial bluff), whether there was an all-in hand initiated, and the amount of money wagered were also recorded. This combination of subjective measures and objective outcomes was then compared to the measured social signaling.

RESULTS For bluffing behavior, we found significant correlations with two types of activity signals: speaking activity and motion activity. For speaking activity, the correlation was $r = -0.68, p = 0.02$, and for motion activity the correlation was $r = -0.65, p = 0.03$. All-in situations, where a player is faced with or has initiated a play that places the rest of their money in jeopardy, produced a strong correlation with variable emphasis (lack of consistency), with $r = 0.67$, $p = 0.025$. "Bad beats," where a player is unexpectedly beaten with a substantial loss due to unusual patterns of card draws, produced correlations with voice activity ($r = 0.70$), motion activity ($r = 0.63$), and variable emphasis ($r = 0.50$), each with $p = 0.05$. The significance figures were unusually large because of the small sample size.

DISCUSSION   Speaking time and motion energy are known to be associated with bluffing in the poker community.[13] When a person is bluffing, they consciously try to reduce all signaling, often ceasing to speak and becoming very still, to avoid giving opponents a reason to call them on their bluff. And this is exactly the relationship we found in the sociometer data.

Most of the bluffing, all-in, and bad beat situations were highly stressful, and it was interesting to see if we could detect stressful situations. We defined a stressful hand as any in which the subject subjectively rated their stress a 7 or above (on a scale of 1 to 10). For this measure, variability in vocal emphasis (lack of consistency) produced the largest correlation ($r = 0.76$, $p = 0.01$).

SUMMARY

In this group of studies examining our work relationships, we have seen how honest signals combine to form identifiable roles such as leading, teaming, and active listening. The signals associated with these roles predict business outcomes, and thus underscore that using honest signals to navigate the murky social waters present in all business activities can be quite beneficial.

Our studies show that displays of active listening play a crucial role in both detecting initial interest in an idea as well as keeping customers satisfied. Similarly, displays of leading form the foundation of how well business pitches and negotiations may proceed. As the business plan experiment forcefully demonstrates, it is not only the content of one's vision but also the style with which that vision is presented that contributes to its future success or failure. Clearly, skill in understanding, displaying, and responding to social signals can bring great advantages.

A central characteristic of human life is the huge amount of time and effort that we spend connecting with other people for information, jobs, friendships, and intimate relationships. Not surprisingly, the thin slices research in social psychology shows that we are good at quickly figuring out when we click with someone and when we are on a different wavelength. As these figures of speech suggest, honest signals play a key role in the process of connecting. The experiments described below explore the use of honest signaling in situations as diverse as dating, getting a job, and meeting others in business settings.

INFORMATION AND FRIENDSHIP

Conferences, mixers, fairs, and meetings are ubiquitous in modern life, each with the purpose of providing opportunities for connecting with other people or organizations. People at these events often talk of resonating or clicking with other people, demonstrations, and exhibits. Can we predict clicking by observing social signaling?

To answer this question, Jon Gips and I[1] collected a day's worth of data from two international meetings held at the MIT Media Lab, using an early version of the sociometer created in collaboration with Joe Paradiso's research group at MIT.[2] One hundred and thirteen subjects wore sociometers throughout the course of the first conference, which ran for approximately 8 hours, for a total of 904 hours of data. In addition to deploying sociometers, we also positioned small infrared beacons at seventy-six project demonstrations. Six months after this first conference, we also instrumented a second conference with eighty-four subjects and ninety-three demonstrations, producing an additional 672 hours of data.

At each conference, the subjects were instructed to press a button on their sociometer badges when they encountered either another badge wearer or a demonstration that they desired to "bookmark." After the conference, the bookmarks were downloaded from the badges, and the contact and demonstration information was emailed to the participants, facilitating further contact and a deeper exploration of personal interests. The sociometers allowed us to see who was talking to whom, note what demonstrations people were stopping to see, and measure how they behaved while they were talking to someone or watching a demonstration.

RESULTS We analyzed these two data sets with the goal of creating two classifiers: one that would predict the bookmarking of badge-to-badge ("badge") encounters, and another that would predict the bookmarking of badge-to-demonstration ("demonstration") encounters. We found strong correlations between the wearers' social signals and the probability that an encounter would be bookmarked for both the badge and demonstration encounters. Badge encounters, in which two subjects traded contact information, showed a significant correlation between activity and the variability of emphasis in both the body movement and audio features.

In contrast, demonstration encounters, in which a subject asked for more information about a project demonstration, showed a different set of correlations. Both audio and body gestures were suppressed just before the subject asked for more information about the project demonstration.

Using these social signals, we found that we could use activity and the variability of emphasis (both audio and body motion) to predict the trading of contact information with a cross-validated accuracy of 82.9 percent. Applying this same predictive model to the data from the second conference yielded a testing accuracy of 74.6 percent. It is amazing to note that these predictions are extremely precise: they are not about *eventually* trading information; they are about trading contact information *within the next two minutes*.

For the demonstration encounters, we found that we could predict requests for additional information with an accuracy of 78.3 percent across both the fall and spring meetings. Again, these predictions were not about eventually asking for more information, they were instead predictions of whether the person would request additional information *within the next two minutes*.

DISCUSSION Our analysis shows that we can automatically predict when people will trade contact information or ask for information with about 80 percent accuracy, without taking into account personal characteristics, history, or other prior knowledge. The intuition behind these results is fairly simple. One might expect that animated conversations would be more likely to result in being bookmarked. Hence, a display of exploring by both people predicts trading contact information. Similarly, one might expect that when people are paying close attention to a demonstration, they would tend to be more quiet and still. And indeed, we find that a period of active listening in front of a demonstration predicts the request for more information.

HIRING DECISIONS

An important type of connection is getting hired for a job. Social science research[3] has confirmed the intuition most of us have: an interviewer's impressions are formed quickly and strongly effect the eventual hiring decision.[4] Therefore, it seems likely that social signaling will predict job hiring.

To test this, Madan measured vocal social signaling during thirty hiring interviews at the MAEER School of Management.[5] The interviews were conducted using the school's standard human resources questionnaire, and lasted for between six and fourteen minutes.

The questionnaire used by the interviewers included the following questions:

1. Please introduce yourself
2. Please give a brief academic background

3. Why did you select engineering?
4. What are your extracurricular interests?
5. What are your future plans?
6. Why do you think I should hire you for my company?

At the end, the interviewers graded the candidates on performance, engagement, confidence, and overall impression.

RESULTS As with the business plan pitches, the ratings in each evaluation category were highly correlated, suggesting that the interviewees' style tended to outweigh other factors. We therefore focused on the overall impression ratings of the candidates. When we compared the ratings of the overall impression to the social signaling measurements, we found that the consistency, mimicry, and influence features accounted for almost 43 percent of the variability of the data, with $r = 0.66$, $p \ll 0.01$.

DISCUSSION The goal of the job applicant is to show that they are attentive to the details of the situation, they care about the job and the challenges it presents, and they are confident of their ability to face those challenges. Consequently, interviewing for a job is perhaps the prototypical experience where one would expect a display of teaming to be effective. These data show that the people who are most likely to get the job are indeed those who displayed attention, empathic understanding, and focused thought and purpose by adopting a style of behavior that includes high influence, ample mimicry, and consistent emphasis and rhythm.

DATING

Depending on who you are, even more important than getting a job may be getting a date. To look at the age-old question, "Will she say yes?" Madan and I conducted a study of social signaling at a real-world speed-dating event.[6] Speed dating is a relatively new way for singles to meet many potential matches in a single evening. The participants interact with their randomly chosen "dates" (other participants) in five-minute sessions. At the end of a session, each individual indicates to the organizers of the event whether they would like to provide contact information to the other person. A "match" occurs when both parties tell the organizers yes, in which case the organizers provide mutual contact information. The data were collected from sixty five-minute speed-dating sessions, where individuals aged twenty-one to forty-five were wearing a sociometer. The vocal social signaling of each individual was then compared to their decision about whether or not to trade contact information.

RESULTS While little correlation appeared between male speaking patterns and attraction (i.e., yes responses), female speaking patterns significantly explained both female ($r = 0.48$, $p = 0.03$) *and* male ($r = 0.50$, $p = 0.02$) attraction. Thus, female social signaling is more important in determining a couple's attraction response than male signaling. For female attraction, the most important factor was high activity, though variable emphasis (low consistency) also played a role. Together, the activity and consistency features produced a classifier with an accuracy of 71 percent in predicting the trading of contact information, as compared to approximately 20 percent accuracy with random guessing.

DISCUSSION We would expect that the exploring display—activity to signal excitement, and variable emphasis to signal openness to further interaction—would be the key to successful dating, and that is what the results of this experiment demonstrate.

It is also unsurprising that only the female signaling was predictive of female behavior. Yet it is interesting that males' offers of contact information were predicted by the female exploring display, since this shows that the males were accurately reading the female display.

SUMMARY

The data from these experiments demonstrate how social signals form the foundation of many of our common social interactions. Decisions as central to our lives as getting a job or getting a date depend on our ability to correctly display as well as interpret a variety of honest signals. These signals are so influential that even a thin slice of signaling can be the determining factor of major life decisions.

People normally use these signals automatically, unconsciously, and continuously. But by becoming more aware of other people's signaling, we can become more adept at reading the social roles that are on display. Because so many of our goals in life require supportive social networks, learning to be better at figuring out when things are clicking and when they are on a different wavelength can have a dramatic effect on one's life.

APPENDIX D: SOCIAL CIRCUITS

The human world is a network of social relationships, composed of networks of work colleagues, friends, neighbors, and dozens of other types of social roles. Networks determine with whom we share, with whom we have social capital, and from whom we stay separate. In a very real sense, social networks constitute our identity.

A critical question, then, is: Who is in which network? This is more difficult to answer than it might appear. First, network connections and the strength of those connections are constantly changing. Second, most of the knowledge we have about network membership is tacit; often people aren't explicitly told about network membership or even think about it. Instead, we see two people talking in a certain way or a certain context, and from that fleeting, thin slice of behavior we infer the connection between them.

So how is it that we know who might be friends with each other, who works together, and so on? It seems that honest social signals are likely to play a major part in our ability to perceive social networks.

DEFINING SOCIAL NETWORKS

What is a social network? People seem to know one when they see one, but it is actually quite difficult to pin down. Social scientists usually use survey data to define a network, using questions like: Do you know them? How often do you see them? They also use email traffic. But surveys are surprisingly inaccurate. During one experiment, for example, we asked the subjects to fill out a daily survey providing a list of their interactions with others. We found only 54 percent agreement between the subjects about having a conversation, and only 29 percent agreed on the number of conversations.[1]

Instead, we will define two people to be connected if they influence the *probability* of each other's behavior, as seen by an outside observer. For instance, if you tell me that John is going to a meeting, and that information raises my estimate of the probability that Mary will be there too, then we will say that John is connected to Mary, at least for the behavior of going to meetings. This does not mean that John's behavior *causes* Mary's behavior, only that there is some predictable connection that relates the two. A social network, then, is a network of people whose behavior somehow connected. The particular behaviors that are connected, be they working, playing, or going to church, define the character of the social network.

These conditional probability connections, which we refer to as influence throughout the book, allow us to predict the behavior of one subject from the other subjects' data. If Joe shows up at a meeting whenever Fred does, for instance, then observing Fred's attendance allows an accurate prediction of Joe's impending proximity.

This sort of influence model is similar to the hidden Markov model commonly used in speech recognition, but there is one important simplification. Instead of keeping the entire set of probabilities about how one person's action might be affected by all of the possible actions of all the other people, the influence model assumes that *how much* one person is influenced by another person's actions is an attribute of the relationship between the two people.

This simplification seems reasonable for the domain of human interactions and potentially for many other domains: we are modeling the strength of the ties (the influence) between people separately from the effects of everyone else's actions. By estimating these influence parameters, we can gain an understanding of how much the people influence each other. The influence model has the advantage that it makes it possible to analyze global behavior while avoiding the exponential number of states typically required by other models of interacting individuals or agents.[2]

MEASURING AFFILIATION

We have talked about exploring displays at conferences, and have shown that we can use the sociometer to predict when people will trade contact information or ask for more details about a demonstration. Can we also tell when people are members of the same social network by observing their social signaling?

To answer this question, Gips and I looked at the sociometer data from two conferences at MIT, described in appendix C.[3] At the first of these conferences, 113 subjects wore sociometers; at the second conference, 84 subjects wore sociometers, producing a total of 1,576 hours of data. The sociometers allowed us to see who was talking to whom, observe where people went, and measure how they behaved during the entire day.

RESULTS Based on the registration data, we knew which people were members of the same company. This information allowed us to compare behavior to company affiliation, and discover which, if any, behaviors were predictive of affiliation. We found two factors, which can be used independently or in combination.

The cumulative time spent face-to-face with someone correlated with whether two people are affiliated or not ($r = 0.47$, $p \ll 0.01$). We could also determine affiliations from similarities between the movements of pairs of subjects. We found the influence values between two people's movements also correlated with being from the same company ($r = 0.3981$, $p \ll 0.01$). Combining the cumulative time and influence predictors using a simple regression model produces a predictor of company affiliation with a cross-validation accuracy of 92.7 percent.

DISCUSSION The intuition here is clear. Two people with the same affiliation probably already know each other, and hence are more likely to spend more time together than two people picked at random. Moreover, they are likely to engage in coordinated behavior, which we can detect by calculating the influence between them. Note that coordinated behavior does *not* mean that they have similar behavior or even correlated behavior; people with the same affiliation are just as likely to split up so that they can cover more of the demonstrations at a conference as they are to walk together. Influence is a much more subtle and accurate indicator of connection than simple similarity.

ANALYZING SOCIAL STRUCTURE

The same methods that we used to detect affiliation using sociometer data can be used to analyze social structure more generally. Today's smart phones can be programmed to keep track of their owners' location and their proximity to other people by sensing cell tower and Bluetooth identifications, respectively. A smart phone therefore becomes a type of sociometer. This has provided us with approximately 330,000 hours of data covering the movement and meeting behavior of ninety-four people, or a total of about thirty-five years of interaction data, as described in Eagle and Pentland.[4]

In our first experiment with this smart phone sociometer data, we measured only coarse location, as determined by which cell tower the subject's phone was connecting through. Each subject's ten most commonly seen cell towers were analyzed, in order to determine when they were at work or at home, and then the influence between people was calculated.

In a second experiment, we used the influence model to analyze the *proximity* between people. Cell phones with Bluetooth radios produce weak signals that include a unique identifier, which is typically detectable at a range of only a few meters. Thus, by looking at the Bluetooth identifications that a cell phone detects, you can determine what other cell phones are around. Since people tend to carry their cell phones everywhere, the proximity of two cell phones is a reliable indicator that the two owners are near to each other.

RESULTS Analysis of the location and proximity data showed that most people follow regular patterns of movement and interpersonal association, and consequently we can predict their movements and meetings with surprising accuracy. We could accurately predict their movements and meetings during the afternoon from their movements and meetings during the morning. We could obtain even greater accuracy at predicting their movements and meetings from observations of the other subjects.

Only a few of the subjects were highly independent and thus not predictable. These subjects were new students, who had not yet picked up the rhythm of the community, and the faculty advisers. The advisers set the pattern of meetings and locations for the students, but their behavior could not be predicted from that of the students.

When we analyzed the influence relationships in the proximity data, we found that clusters of influence map cleanly to our notion of affiliation and friendship. Just as seen in the sociometer data taken during a conference, the influence observed between people revealed the structure of the social network. Clustering the daytime influence relationships allowed 96 percent accuracy at identifying work group affiliation, and clustering the evening influence relationships produced 92 percent accuracy at identifying self-reported close friendships.[5]

DISCUSSION The ability to accurately characterize people's social networks by measuring their interpersonal influence (conditional probability structure) means that we can automatically determine subjects' social network membership with high accuracy. Moreover, this automatic labeling of relationships works even for dynamically changing social networks; its accuracy is largely a function of the amount of observation data available.

CONNECTORS IN SOCIAL NETWORKS

We have seen that we can use influence between people's movements and proximity to determine their affiliation and map social networks. Does this influence relationship also apply to finer-grain behaviors, like conversational turn taking and social signaling?

Tanzeem Choudhury and I used sociometers to collect vocal social signaling from twenty-three subjects from four different research groups over a period of eleven days, resulting in an average of 66 hours of data per subject, for a total of 1,518 hours of data.[6] The subjects were a representative sample of the community, including students, faculty, and administrative staff. During data collection, users wore a sociometer for 6 hours a day (11:00 a.m. to 5:00 p.m.) while they were on the MIT campus.

We then selected eighty conversations that were an average of five minutes long to compute the individual turn-taking dynamics. In selecting the conversations, we made sure that we had at least four different conversational partners for each individual and multiple conversational instances for the same conversational pair, resulting in a total of seventeen subjects for whom we could accurately quantify their conversational dynamics. Of these seventeen subjects, ten had at least four different conversational partners, allowing us to estimate not only their mean behavior but also how they change or are influenced by other people's interaction behavior. These changes in behavior were compared to the subjects' *betweenness centrality*, which measures how much control an individual has over the interaction of other individuals who are not directly connected.[7] People with high betweenness are frequently viewed as leaders.

RESULTS Our first finding was that the statistics describing individuals' turn-taking styles are distinctive and stable across different conversational partners, and that these turn-taking patterns are not just a noisy variation of an overall, average style ($p \ll 0.01$). Since these statistics determine the average values of the activity and influence measures, the implication is that people have characteristic styles of activity and influence signaling. These styles are related to subjective properties such as extraversion and charisma.

Interestingly, male and female patterns were different, with only slight overlap between the range of parameters observed for males and those observed for females. Surprisingly, the total speaking time for males and females was nearly equal, however men's utterances were typically longer than those of women.

Perhaps the most important finding was that people's characteristic influence style was an accurate predictor of the person's betweenness centrality, a standard social science measure of how important an individual is to the information flow within a social network. The correlation value between this centrality measure and the influence parameter was $r = 0.90$, $p \ll 0.01$ Thus, the amount of influence that an individual had on other people's turn-taking style was a nearly perfect predictor of how much of a connector they were.

DISCUSSION Just as influence allowed us to classify affiliation and map the social network, it also allowed us to determine people's importance to the information flow in the social network. Our discovery that a property of the entire network can be seen in the behavior of each individual demonstrates that we are deeply connected to the global structure of our social network. Furthermore, this process is unconscious; none of the subjects were aware that they spoke differently to the connectors, nor were they even able to name who the connectors were.

SUMMARY

These studies looked beyond one-to-one social interactions to explore the larger worlds of social networks. Central to this is the not-so-simple task of defining who is actually in a network, and measuring the strength of people's interactions with the network.

We have constructed a method of measuring interpersonal influence that has allowed us to *automatically* map social networks from simple observations of objective behavior. That is, by observing patterns of proximity or conversational turn taking, we can accurately map the org chart of an organization or community.

The same method lets us estimate a given person's importance to the flow of information within that network. We can map out who is central and even who sets the pattern of communication. This type of "information influence map" is likely to prove to be the key to tailoring an organization's pattern of communication to be more effective and efficient.

In the near future, we envision a new generation of management tools that are enabled by the sociometer's capability to produce real-time maps of an organization's information flow and function. These sensible organizations will use these new sensing capabilities to make sure that the sales department really is talking to the marketing department, and that employees aren't overloaded and miserable. To achieve this it will take special care to strike a balance between the "big brother" nature of such information and the benefits that can be reaped. We believe that this balance can be achieved by giving employees control of their own information, creating a transparent system with immediate benefits to everyone.

APPENDIX E: UNCONSCIOUS INTELLIGENCE

This book has argued that groups of early humans could make intelligent decisions despite the lack of sophisticated language by using the mechanism of network intelligence—that is, by creating an idea market using social signaling. It seems, however, that we need a similar explanatory framework for individual humans as well; our reasoning powers often appear so limited that they seem incapable of producing intelligent decisions.

The Nobel Prize–winning work of Daniel Kahneman and Amos Tversky demonstrated that people are at best "boundedly rational."[1] That is, in our normal day-to-day life, our actions and beliefs fail to follow even the simplest logical rules. Even experts have an incredibly limited ability to predict outcomes, as carefully detailed in Philip Tetlock's study of how often experts' predictions turn out to be true.[2] He recorded and then followed up on expert predictions for more than twenty years, and found that experts are often little better than novices at making predictions. Surprisingly, the most famous experts tend to be the worst of all.

CONSCIOUS AND UNCONSCIOUS

If these findings about our decision-making abilities were from apes or other animals, they would hardly raise an eyebrow. After all, everyone knows that animals don't think too much and generally act on instinct. So could the same be true of people also? Perhaps consciousness isn't as important as we usually think. We may need to reexamine our assumptions about how much of a role both conscious and unconscious forces play in shaping our day-to-day behaviors. Our sociometer data support the view that a great deal of human behavior is either automatic or determined by unconscious processes. This is not to say that conscious processes do not play a role; rather, the balance may be tipped in favor of unconscious processes in the majority of our daily activities.

A recent report in *Science* by Ap Dijksterhuis and his colleagues, for instance, showed that unconscious thinking is frequently more effective than conscious thought.[3] They compared people making conscious decisions with those who made their choice based on their unconscious "gut instinct." What they found was that for simple tasks, people acting consciously make better decisions, but for more complex problems, acting on unconscious instinct was far more effective. The reason, they suggest, is that conscious thinking cannot cope with many trade-offs at once, whereas unconscious thinking can integrate lots of information together to make an overall judgment.

As Buchanan, a former editor of *Nature*, points out, if unconscious thinking comes into its own whenever we face information
overload, it is hardly surprising that we use it so much in our
complex social interactions.[4] In fact, this may be its most important
sphere of influence.

RECOGNIZING THE TRUTH

So how might this unconscious decision making work? Perhaps the
best guess is that our unconscious decision-making abilities are
based on those skills where we excel, and what we are really masters
at is remembering events and recognizing patterns. Herbert Simon,
the Nobel laureate psychologist, noted that intuition (that is, unconscious decision making) is nothing more and nothing less than recognition.[5] People are surprisingly good at making qualitative
estimates about how likely events are. If we think about expert poker
players again, we see that they are good at recognizing what patterns
of play are unfolding as well as predicting how likely future draws
of cards are to be favorable (just don't ask for logical consistency).

Thomas Griffiths and Joshua Tenenbaum recently found that
people are strikingly good at this sort of classification and estima-
tion even for topics where they are not experts.[6] One intriguing
example showed that even college-age males collectively have good
intuitions about how long cake mixes take to bake, and that there
are two types of cakes with different baking times—although they
couldn't put these intuitions into words, and may have never even
baked a cake.

So how can we use this rather amazing individual ability
to remember similar events and estimate odds to build idea

markets in support of individual intelligence? Let's begin by examining the parallels between network intelligence and individual intelligence.

The idea of network intelligence is that action selection arises from the coordination of individual minds through social circuits, just as individual intelligence arises from the coordination of specialized brain centers through neural circuits. In network intelligence, this coordination uses interest, typically signaled by activity, as a way for individuals to bet on various alternative actions. After being weighted by the individuals' records for successful betting, the bets are summed together, and the course of action with the most bets is selected. When structured correctly, this signaling mechanism can successfully integrate different sources of information while avoiding the problems of idiots and gossip.

We can imagine a similar mechanism within individual minds, giving us the ability to "see the truth" by using "internal perception" to examine our memories, retrieve those that are similar, and estimate the odds. We can imagine a brain mechanism whereby each alternative action receives activation in proportion to its recognizability—that is, by how similar it is to past situations. The emotions attached to each action might serve as the rating of the actions' past outcomes, so that actions that have turned out poorly in the past are given little weight. Thus, activation from recognition of similar situations, weighted by the outcomes associated with those memories, serves to place a bet on each alternative action. These weighted activities are then summed together, and the course of action with the most activation is selected.

So perhaps individual intelligence arises from the coordination of memories through neural circuits, in much the same manner as network intelligence can arise from the coordination of individual minds through social circuits. In network intelligence, this coordination may employ interest, typically signaled by activity, as a way for individuals to bet on various alternative actions. In individual intelligence, betting through neural activation could play the same role of selecting among different memories of actions. This type of action selection mechanism, interestingly, is commonly used in robotics, where it usually functions well. Robotics has also demonstrated its usefulness within group situations; it has been used successfully in some teams of robots to play soccer against other teams.

SUMMARY

The most startling point made by this research is that decision making isn't about logic or rational argument. We just don't seem to be good at this sort of reasoning, no matter how hard we try. The major sorts of problems we encounter aren't errors in logic—those are detectable and thus fixable—but the difficulty of accurately capturing the full complexity of the world in linguistic statements and mathematical models.

The second point that comes from this research is that there are no superpowered experts who are smarter than all the rest of us. Sometimes experts have a run of luck and get it right several times in a row, but their odds on the next problem are no better than the next guy. Moreover, the best experts are broad rather than deep, which makes them harder to package into a sound bite, and hence they tend to be less well-known. We need to wean ourselves from the "big man" theory of management.

So then how does all this evidence help us make better decisions? What the evidence and model suggest is that for complex problems, the best decision-making strategy is to focus on information discovery and then let your unconscious mind "recognize" the best alternative.

Pragmatically, this means beginning by reaching out into your social network to learn about as many related situations as possible. Experience—especially broad experience—counts. Then you should carefully consider how similar each is to the current situation and how the features of each example are related to the outcomes. Remember especially the problem of gossip: similar examples count as one alternative, not many alternatives.

And finally, let the problem roll around in your mind without conscious deliberation. Don't look for a logical explanation of every factor but instead seek that "aha" moment where you recognize a real fit between your current problem and previous experience. An informed unconscious, especially one supported by the experiences of a network of interested individuals, is the most powerful decision-making tool you have.

NOTES

PREFACE: A GOD'S EYE VIEW

1. Olguin, Paradiso, and Pentland 2006; see also appendix A.

2. See appendix B.

3. Baker and Faulkner 2004.

4. Pentland 2007c.

5. Pentland et al. 2005; Pentland 2005.

6. Pentland 2005, 2007a.

7. Pentland 2007c.

8. Pentland 2004; see also appendixes A, B, C, and D.

9. Zahavi and Zahavi 1997; Lachmann, Szamado, and Bergstrom 2001.

10. Bird, Smith, and Bird 2001; Godfray and Johnstone 2000.

CHAPTER 1   HONEST SIGNALS

1. Madan and Pentland 2006; see also appendix C.

2. Zahavi and Zahavi 1997; Godfray and Johnstone 2000; Lachmann, Szamado, and Bergstrom 2001; Bird, Smith, and Bird 2001.

3. Coelho and McClure 1993.

4. Frackowiak 2004.

5. Rizzolatti and Craighero 2004; Iacoboni and Mazziotta 2007.

6. Gershon 1998.

7. Sung and Pentland 2005; Fraguas et al. 2007.

8. Frackowiak 2004.

9. Provine 2001.

10. Handel 1989; Werner and Keller 1994; Nass and Brave 2004.

11. Pendergast 1990.

12. Gregory and Galeasher 2002.

13. Fernald and Mazzie 1991; Jaffe et al. 2001.

14. Roy and Pentland 2002.

15. Cohn and Tronick 1988; Jaffe et al. 2001.

16. Kaplan, Bachorowski, and Zarlengo-Strouse 1999; Kaplan et al. 2002; Kaplan, Dungan and Zinser 2004.

17. Pentland 2004; Curhan and Pentland 2007.

18. Chartrand and Bargh 1999; Chartrand, Maddux, and Lakin 2005; Tummolini et al. 2006.

19. Gallese and Goldman 1998.

20. Chartrand, Maddux, and Lakin 2005.

21. Bailenson and Yee 2005.

22. Curhan and Pentland 2007; see also appendix B.

23. Gershon 1998.

24. Madan and Pentland 2006; see also appendix C.

25. Madan and Pentland 2006; see also appendix B.

26. Gips and Pentland 2006; see also appendix C.

27. Werner and Keller 1994; Nass and Brave 2004.

28. Verwey and Veltman 1996; O'Donnell and Eggemeier 1986.

29. Curhan and Pentland 2007; see also appendix B.

30. Stoltzman 2006; see also appendix B.

31. Stoltzman 2006; see also appendix B.

32. Basu 2002.

33. See also appendixes B and C.

34. Conradt and Roper 2005; Couzin et al. 2005; Dunbar 1996.

CHAPTER 2   SOCIAL ROLES

1. Curhan and Pentland 2007; see also appendix B.

2. See also appendixes B and C.

3. Gips and Pentland 2006; see also appendix C.

4. Madan and Pentland 2006; see also appendix C.

5. Gips and Pentland 2006; see also appendix C.

6. Stoltzman 2006; see also appendix B.

7. Sung and Pentland 2005; see also appendix B.

8. Curhan and Pentland 2007; see also appendix B.

9. Madan and Pentland 2006; see also appendix C.

10. Curhan and Pentland 2007; see also appendix B.

11. Stoltzman 2006; see also appendix B.

12. Ambady and Rosenthal 1992.

13. Pentland 2004.

14. Pentland 2007c; see also appendix E.

15. Dow et al. 2007.

16. Madan and Pentland 2006.

CHAPTER 3   READING PEOPLE

1. Sung and Pentland 2005; see also appendix B.

2. Whiten et al. 1999; Hauser 2005.

3. Conradt and Roper 2005.

4. DeWaal 2005.

5. Pentland 2004, 2007c.

6. Bikhchandani, Hirshleifer, and Welch 1998; Goldstone and Janssen 2005; Axelrod 1997.

7. Rizzolatti and Craighero 2004; Iacoboni and Mazziotta 2007.

8. Gallese and Goldman 1998; Tummolini et al. 2006.

9. Roy and Pentland 2002; Fernald and Mazzie 1991.

10. Bikhchandani, Hirshleifer, and Welch 1998.

11. Barsade 2002.

12. Greer 2005.

13. Bono and Ilies 2006.

14. Iacoboni and Mazziotta 2007.

15. Bailenson and Yee 2005.

16. Chartrand and Bargh 1999; Chartrand, Maddux, and Lakin 2005.

17. Pentland 2004.

18. Barsade 2002; Reicher, Haslam, and Platow 2007.

19. Brinol and Petty 2003.

CHAPTER 4 SURVIVAL SIGNALS

1. Hall and Watson 1970.

2. Bales 1970. Normally these are called "social roles," but to avoid confusion with the social roles conveyed by honest signaling, we will call these "group roles."

3. Pianesi et al. forthcoming.

4. Brown 1986; Janis 1972; Baron 2005.

5. Pianesi et al. forthcoming.

6. Dong et al. 2007.

7. Hoffman 1979; Mowday 1981.

8. Madan and Pentland 2006; see also appendix B.

9. Gatica-Perez et al. 2005.

10. Wilson, Timmel, and Miller 2004.

11. Gatica-Perez et al. 2005.

12. Barsade 2002.

13. Hackman 2002; Bono and Ilies 2006.

14. Bono and Ilies 2006.

15. Hackman 2002; Reicher, Haslam, and Platow 2007.

16. Milgram 1974.

17. Haney, Banks and Zimbardo 1973.

18. Kim and Pentland 2007.

CHAPTER 5   NETWORK INTELLIGENCE

1. Buchanan 2007b; Wilson 2002.

2. Conradt and Roper 2005.

3. Stewart and Harcourt 1994.

4. Boinski and Campbell 1995.

5. Conradt and Roper 2005; Couzin et al. 2005; Couzin 2007.

6. Kambil 2003; Chen, Fine, and Huberman 2004.

7. Hoffman 1979; Mowday 1981.

8. Gatica-Perez et al. 2005; Madan and Pentland 2006; see also appendix B.

9. Brown 1986; Janis 1972; Chen, Fine, and Huberman 2003; Baron 2005.

10. Chen, Fine, and Huberman 2003, 2004.

11. Prelec 2004.

12. Chilongo 2006.

13. Barsade 2002; Bono and Ilies 2006.

14. Hackman 2002; Reicher, Haslam, and Platow 2007.

15. Dunbar 1996.

16. Wilson 2002.

CHAPTER 6   SENSIBLE ORGANIZATIONS

1. Conradt and Roper 2005.

2. For an example of signaling in hunter-gatherer societies, see Bird, Smith, and Bird 2001.

3. Buchanan 2007b, Wilson 2002.

4. See also appendix D.

5. Ancona, Bresman, and Kaeufer 2002.

6. Bavelas 1950.

7. Kidane and Gloor 2007.

8. Waber et al. 2007.

9. Gloor et al. 2007.

10. Eagle and Pentland 2006; Dong and Pentland 2007.

11. Oliver, Rosario, and Pentland 2000.

12. Freeman 1977, 1978–1979.

13. See also appendix D.

14. Dong and Pentland 2006.

15. Waber et al. 2007.

16. Waber et al. 2007.

17. Eagle 2006, Eagle and Pentland 2006.

18. Handy 1995; Early and Gibson 2002.

19. Hackman 2002; Reicher, Haslam, and Platow 2007.

20. Pentland et al. 2005; Ara et al. 2006; Olguin, Paradiso, and Pentland 2006; Buchanan 2007a.

CHAPTER 7   SENSIBLE SOCIETIES

1. Goldstone and Janssen 2005.

2. Axelrod 1997; Putnam 1975; Wegner 1995.

3. Haney, Banks, and Zimbardo 1973; Milgram 1974; Bikhchandani, Hirshleifer, and Welch 1998; Lazer 2001; Chartrand and Bargh 1999; Asch 1955.

4. Brown 1991.

5. Goldstone and Janssen 2005; Conradt and Roper 2005; Couzin et al. 2005; Couzin 2007; Boinski and Campbell 1995; Stewart and Harcourt 1994.

6. Ancona, Bresman, and Kaeufer 2002.

7. Harris 1995.

8. Pentland et al. 2005; Pentland 2004; Ara et al. 2006; Buchanan 2007a; Olguin, Paradiso, and Pentland 2006.

9. Buchanan 2007a, 2007b.

10. Dong and Pentland 2006.

11. Eagle 2006, Eagle and Pentland 2006.

EPILOGUE: TECHNOLOGY AND SOCIETY

1. Pentland 2005.

2. Pentland 2007b.

APPENDIX A: SOCIAL SCIENCE BACKGROUND

1. Ambady and Rosenthal 1993; Allport 1937; Funder and Colvin 1988; Gladwell 2005; Goffman 1979.

2. For a review, see Wright 1969.

3. Webster and Anderson 1964.

4. Blanck et al. 1986.

5. Borkenau et al. 2004.

6. Blanck, Rosenthal, and Cordell 1985; for reviews, see Ambady, Bernieri, and Richeson 2000; Ambady and Rosenthal 1992.

7. For a review, see Gottman and Notarius 2000.

8. Carrere and Gottman 1999.

9. Ambady and Rosenthal 1992.

10. Rosenthal and Rubin 1982.

11. Coelho and McClure 1993.

12. Ambady and Rosenthal 1992; Nass and Brave 2004.

13. Dunbar 1996; Provine 2001.

14. Choudhury and Pentland 2004.

15. Choudbury and Pentland 2004; Laibowitz et al. 2006; Olguin, Paradiso, and Pentland 2006.

16. Olguin, Paradiso, and Pentland 2006.

17. Note that this terminology has evolved since some of our earlier papers; we used to say stress instead of consistency, and engagement instead of influence. These terms proved too confusing to readers, and so have been changed.

18. Valbonesi et al. 2002.

19. Mast 2002.

20. Bottger 1984; Littlepage et al. 1995.

21. Jaffe et al. 2001; Thomas and Malone 1979.

22. Jaffe et al. 2001.

23. Werner and Keller 1994; Handel 1989.

24. Fernald and Mazzie 1991.

25. Frick 1985.

26. Verwey and Veltman 1996; O'Donnell and Eggemeier 1986.

27. Chartrand and Bargh 1999.

28. For a review, see Chartrand, Maddux, and Lakin 2005.

29. Van Baaren et al. 2003.

30. Picard 1997.

31. Cassell 2000.

32. Zahavi and Zahavi 1997; Godfray and Johnstone 2000; Bird, Smith, and Bird 2001.

33. Chartrand and Bargh 1999; Ambady and Rosenthal 1992.

34. Gladwell 2005.

APPENDIX B: SUCCESS

1. Madan and Pentland 2006.

2. Stoltzman 2006.

3. Rosenberg and Hirschberg 2005.

4. Stoltzman 2006.

5. More precisely, the standard deviation of the spectral entropy, the average length of a speaking segment, voicing rate, and the call duration.

6. In this case the standard deviation of energy, the average length of a speaking segment, and the call duration.

7. Curhan and Pentland 2007.

8. Campbell and Kashy 2002.

9. Kashy and Kenny 2000.

10. Pentland 2004.

11. Tiedens and Fragale 2003.

12. Sung and Pentland 2005.

13. Caro 2003.

APPENDIX C: CONNECTING

1. Gips and Pentland 2006.

2. Laibowitz et al. 2006.

3. For a review, see Wright 1969.

4. Webster and Anderson 1964; Webster 1982.

5. Madan 2006.

6. Madan and Pentland 2006.

APPENDIX D: SOCIAL CIRCUITS

1. Choudhury and Pentland 2004.

2. Pentland et al. 2005; Dong and Pentland 2006, 2007.

3. Gips and Pentland 2006.

4. Eagle and Pentland 2006.

5. Dong and Pentland 2007; see also Eagle and Pentland 2006 for another method of inferring friendships.

6. Choudhury and Pentland 2004.

7. Freeman 1977.

APPENDIX E: UNCONSCIOUS INTELLIGENCE

1. Kahneman and Tversky 1979.

2. Tetlock 2005.

3. Dijksterhuis et al. 2006.

4. Buchanan 2007c.

5. Simon 1995.

6. Griffiths and Tenenbaum 2006.

REFERENCES

Allport, G. W. 1937. *Personality: A psychological interpretation.* New York: H. Holt and Co.

Ambady, N., F. J. Bernieri, and J. A. Richeson. 2000. Toward a histology of social behavior: Judgmental accuracy from thin slices of the behavioral stream. *Advances in Experimental Social Psychology* 32: 201–257.

Ambady, N., and R. Rosenthal. 1992. Thin slices of expressive behavior as predictors of interpersonal consequences: A meta-analysis. *Psychological Bulletin* 111, no. 2 (March): 256–274.

Ambady, N., and R. Rosenthal. 1993. Half a minute: Predicting teacher evaluations from thin slices of nonverbal behavior and physical attractiveness. *Journal of Personality and Social Psychology* 64 (33): 431–441.

Ancona, D., H. Bresman, and K. Kaeufer. 2002. The comparative advantage of x-teams. *MIT Sloan Management Review* 43, no. 3 (Spring): 33–40.

Ara, K., H. Kanehira, E. Megally, Y. Poltorak, G. Singh, R. Smith, D. Suzuki, M. Mortensen, M. Van Alstyne, and A. Pentland. 2006. Sensible organization inspired by social sensor technologies. *MIT Media Lab Technical Report* 602. See <http://hd.media.mit.edu>.

Asch, S. E. 1955. Opinions and social pressures. *Scientific American* 193, no. 5 (November): 31–35.

Axelrod, R. 1997. The dissemination of culture: A model with local convergence and global polarization. *Journal of Conflict Resolution* 41 (2): 203–226.

Bailenson, J., and N. Yee. 2005. Digital chameleons: Automatic assimilation of nonverbal gestures in immersive virtual environments. *Psychological Science* 16, no. 10 (October): 814–819.

Baker, W., and R. Faulkner. 2004. Social networks and loss of capital. *Social Networks* 26: 91–111.

Bales, R. F. 1970. *Personality and interpersonal behavior.* New York: Holt, Rinehart and Winston.

Baron, R. S. 2005. So right it's wrong: Groupthink and the ubiquitous nature of polarized group decision making. *Advances in Experimental Psychology* 37: 219–253.

Barsade, S. 2002. The ripple effect: Emotional contagion and its influence on group behavior. *Administrative Science Quarterly* 47 (4): 644–675.

Basu, S. 2002. Conversational scene analysis. PhD thesis, MIT. See <http://hd.media.mit.edu>.

Bavelas, A. 1950. Communication patterns in task-oriented groups. *Journal of the Acoustical Society of America* 22 (6): 725–730.

Bikhchandani, S., D. Hirshleifer, and I. Welch. 1998. Learning from the behavior of others: Conformity, fads, and informational cascades. *Journal of Economic Perspectives* 12 (3): 151–170.

Bird, R., E. Smith, and D. Bird. 2001. The hunting handicap: Costly signaling in human foraging strategies. *Behavioral Ecology and Sociobiology* 50 (1): 9–19.

Blanck, P. D., R. Rosenthal, and L. H. Cordell. 1985. The appearance of justice: Judges' verbal and nonverbal behavior in criminal jury trials. *Stanford Law Review* 38 (November): 89–164.

Blanck, P. D., R. Rosenthal, M. Vannicelli, and T. D. Lee. 1986. Therapists' tone of voice: Descriptive, psychometric, interactional, and competence analyses. *Journal of Social and Clinical Psychology* 4 (2): 154–178.

Boinski, S., and A. F. Campbell. 1995. Use of trill vocalizations to coordinate troop movement among white-faced capuchins: A second field test. *Behaviour* 132 (11–12): 875–901.

Bono, J., and R. Ilies. 2006. Charisma, positive emotions, and mood contagion. *Leadership Quarterly* 17, no. 4 (August): 317–334.

Borkenau, P., N. Mauer, R. Riemann, F. M. Spinath, and A. Angleitner. 2004. Thin slices of behavior as cues of personality and intelligence. *Journal of Personality and Social Psychology* 86 (4): 599–614.

Bottger, P. C. 1984. Expertise and air time as bases of actual and perceived influence in problem-solving groups. *Journal of Applied Psychology* 69 (2): 214–221.

Briñol, P., and R. E. Petty. 2003. Overt head movements and persuasion: A self-validation analysis. *Journal of Personality and Social Psychology* 84: 1123–1139.

Brown, D. E. 1991. *Human universals*. New York: McGraw-Hill.

Brown, R. 1986. Group polarization. In *Social psychology*, ed. R. Brown, 200–248. 2nd ed. New York: Free Press.

Buchanan, M. 2007a. The science of subtle signals. *Strategy+Business* 48: 68–77.

Buchanan, M. 2007b. *The social atom: Why the rich get richer, cheaters get caught, and your neighbor usually looks like you.* New York: Bloomsbury.

Buchanan, M. 2007c. What made you read this? *New Scientist*, July 7, 36–39.

Campbell, L., and D. A. Kashy. 2002. Estimating actor, partner, and interaction effects for dyadic data using PROC MIXED and HLM: A user-friendly guide. *Personal Relationships* 9 (3): 327–342.

Caro, M. 2003. *Caro's book of poker tells.* New York: Cardoza Publishing.

Carrère, S., and J. M. Gottman. 1999. Predicting divorce among newlyweds from the first three minutes of a marital conflict discussion. *Family Process* 38: 293–301.

Cassell, J. 2000. Embodied conversational interface agents. *Communications of the ACM* 43 (4): 70–79.

Chartrand, T. L., and J. Bargh. 1999. The chameleon effect: The perception-behavior link and social interaction. *Journal of Personality and Social Psychology* 76 (6): 893–910.

Chartrand, T. L., W. Maddux, and J. Lakin. 2005. Beyond the perception-behavior link: The ubiquitous utility and motivational moderators of nonconscious mimicry. In *The new unconscious*, ed. R. Hassin, J. Uleman, and J. A. Bargh, 334–361. New York: Oxford University Press.

Chen, K. Y., L. Fine, and B. Huberman. 2003. Predicting the future. *Information Systems Frontiers* 5 (1): 47–61.

Chen, K. Y., L. Fine, and B. Huberman. 2004. Eliminating public knowledge biases in information-aggregation mechanisms. *Management Science* 50 (7): 983–994.

Chilongo, D. M. 2006. Social network effects on information aggregation. Masters thesis, MIT. See <http://hd.media.mit.edu>.

Choudhury, T., and A. Pentland. 2004. Characterizing social networks using the sociometer. *Proceedings of the North American Association of Computational Social and Organizational Science*, Pittsburgh, PA, June 10–12. See <http://hd.media.mit.edu>.

Coelho, P., and J. McClure. 1993. Toward an economic theory of fashion. *Economic Inquiry* 31 (4): 595–608.

Cohn, J., and E. Tronick. 1988. Mother-infant face-to-face interaction: Influence is bidirectional and unrelated to periodic cycles in either partner's behavior. *Developmental Psychology* 24 (3): 386–392.

Conradt, L., and T. Roper. 2005. Consensus decision making in animals. *Trends in Ecology and Evolution* 20 (8): 449–456.

Couzin, I. 2007. Collective minds. *Nature* 445, no. 7129 (February 15): 715.

Couzin, I., J. Krause, N. Franks, and S. Levin. 2005. Effective leadership and decision-making in animal groups on the move. *Nature* 433, no. 7025 (February 3): 513–516.

Curhan, J., and A. Pentland. 2007. Thin slices of negotiation: Predicting outcomes from conversational dynamics within the first five minutes. *Journal of Applied Psychology* 92 (3): 802–811. See <http://hd.media.mit.edu>.

De Waal, F. 2005. *Our inner ape*. New York: Riverhead.

Dijksterhuis, A., M. Bos, O. Nordgren, and R. van Baaren. 2006. On making the right choice: The deliberation-without-attention effect. *Science* 311, no. 5763 (February 17): 1005–1007.

Dong, W., B. Lepri, A. Cappelletti, A. Pentland, F. Pianesi, and M. Zancanaro. 2007. Using the influence model to recognize functional roles in meetings. *Proceedings of the ninth International Conference on Multimodal Interfaces*, Nagoya, Japan, November 12–15. See <http://hd.media.mit.edu>.

Dong, W., and A. Pentland. 2006. Multi-sensor data fusion using the influence model. *IEEE Body Sensor Networks*, 72–75, Boston, April 3–5. See <http://hd.media.mit.edu>.

Dong, W., and A. Pentland. 2007. Modeling influence between experts. In *Lecture notes on artificial intelligence: Special volume on human computing*, 4451: 170–189. Berlin: Springer-Verlag.

Dow, A., D. Leong, A. Anderson, R. Wenzel, and VCU Theater-Medicine Team. 2007. Using theater to teach clinical empathy: A pilot study. *Journal of General Internal Medicine* 22 (8): 1114–1118.

Dunbar, R. 1996. *Grooming, gossip, and the evolution of language.* Cambridge, MA: Harvard University Press.

Eagle, N. 2006. Machine perception and learning of complex social systems. PhD diss., MIT. See <http://hd.media.mit.edu>.

Eagle, N., and A. Pentland. 2006. Reality mining: Sensing complex social systems. *Personal and Ubiquitous Computing* 10 (4): 255–268. See <http://hd.media.mit.edu>.

Early, P. C., and C. B. Gibson. 2002. *Multinational work teams: A new perspective.* Mahwah, NJ: Lawrence Erlbaum Associates.

Fernald, A., and C. Mazzie. 1991. Prosody and focus in speech to infants and adults. *Developmental Psychology* 27 (2): 209–221.

Frackowiak, R. 2004. *Human brain function.* 2nd ed. Boston: Elsevier Academic Press.

Fraguas, R., Jr., C. Marci, M. Fava, D. V. Iosifescu, B. Bankier, R. Loh, and D. D. Dougherty. 2007. Autonomic reactivity to induced emotion as potential predictor of response to antidepressant treatment. *Psychiatry Research* 151 (1–2): 169–172.

Freeman, L. C. 1977. A set of measures of centrality based upon betweenness. *Sociometry* 40, no. 1 (March): 35–41.

Freeman, L. C. 1978–1979. Centrality in social networks: Conceptual clarification. *Social Networks* 1: 215–239.

Frick, R. W. 1985. Communicating emotion: The role of prosodic features. *Psychological Bulletin* 97 (3): 412–429.

Funder, D. C., and C. R. Colvin. 1988. Friends and strangers: Acquaintanceship, agreement, and the accuracy of personality judgment. *Journal of Personality and Social Psychology* 55, no. 1 (July): 149–158.

Gallese, V., and A. Goldman. 1998. Mirror neurons and the simulation theory of mind-reading. *Trends in Cognitive Science* 2 (12): 493–501.

Gatica-Perez, D., I. McCowan, D. Zhang, and S. Bengio. 2005. Detecting group interest-level in meetings. *ICASSP*, I-489–I-492.

Gershon, M. D. 1998. *The second brain.* New York: HarperCollins Publishers.

Gips, J., and A. Pentland. 2006. Mapping human networks. *Proceedings of the IEEE International Conference on Pervasive Computing and Communications*, Pisa, Italy, March 13–17. See <http://hd.media.mit.edu>.

Gladwell, M. 2005. *Blink: The power of thinking without thinking.* New York: Little Brown.

Gloor, P., D. Oster, O. Raz, and A. Pentland. 2007. The virtual mirror: Reflecting your social and psychological self to increase organizational creativity. Working paper. See <http://hd.media.mit.edu>.

Godfray, H., and R. A. Johnstone. 2000. Begging and bleating: The evolution of parent-offspring signaling. *Philosophical Transactions B* 355: 1581–1592.

Goffman, E. 1979. *Gender advertisements.* New York: Harper and Row.

Goldstone, R., and M. Janssen. 2005. Computational models of collective behavior. *Trends in Cognitive Science* 9 (9): 424–430.

Gottman, J. M., and C. I. Notarius. 2000. Decade review: Observing marital interaction. *Journal of Marriage and Family* 62, no. 4 (November): 927–947.

Greer, M. 2005. The science of savoir faire. *Monitor on Psychology* 36, no. 1 (January): 28–30.

Gregory, S. W., and T. J. Galeasher. 2002. Spectral analysis of candidates' nonverbal vocal communication: Predicting US presidential election outcomes. *Social Psychology Quarterly* 65: 298–308.

Griffiths, T., and J. Tenenbaum. 2006. Optimal predictions in everyday cognition. *Psychological Science* 17 (9): 767–773.

Hackman, J. R. 2002. *Leading teams: Setting the stage for great performances.* Boston: Harvard Business School Press.

Hall, J. W., and W. H. Watson. 1970. The effects of a normative intervention on group decision-making performance. *Human Relations* 23 (4): 299–317.

Handel, S. 1989. *Listening: An introduction to the perception of auditory events.* Cambridge, MA: MIT Press.

Handy, C. 1995. Trust and the virtual organization. *Harvard Business Review* 73, no. 3 (May–June): 40–48.

Haney, C., W. Banks, and P. Zimbardo. 1973. Interpersonal dynamics in a simulated prison. *International Journal of Criminology and Penology* 1: 69–97.

Harris, J. 1995. Where is the child's environment? A group socialization theory of development. *Psychological Review* 102 (3): 458–489.

Hauser, M. 2005. Our chimpanzee mind. *Nature* 437: 60–63.

Hoffman, L. R. 1979. *The group problem solving process: Studies of a valence model.* New York: Praeger.

Iacoboni, M., and J. C. Mazziotta. 2007. Mirror neuron system: Basic findings and clinical applications. *Annals of Neurology* 62, no. 3 (September): 207–306.

Jaffe, J., B. Beebe, S. Feldstein, C. L. Crown, and M. Jasnow. 2001. Rhythms of dialogue in early infancy. *Monographs of the Society for Research in Child Development* 66 (2): 264.

Janis, I. L. 1972. *Victims of groupthink*. Boston: Houghton Mifflin Company.

Kahneman, D., and A. Tversky. 1979. Prospect theory: An analysis of decisions under risk. *Econometrica* 47, no. 2 (March): 263–292.

Kambil, A. 2003. You can bet on idea markets. *HBS Working Knowledge for Business Leaders*, December. See <http://hbswk.hbs.edu/archive/3808 .html>.

Kaplan, P., J. Bachorowski, M. J. Smoski, and W. Hudenko. 2002. Infants of depressed mothers, although competent learners, fail to learn in response to their own mothers' infant-directed speech. *Psychological Science* 13, no. 3 (May): 268–271.

Kaplan, P., J. Bachorowski, and P. Zarlengo-Strouse. 1999. Child-directed speech produced by mothers with symptoms of depression fails to promote associative learning in 4-month-old infants. *Child Development* 70, no. 3 (May–June): 560–570.

Kaplan, P., J. Dungan, and M. Zinser. 2004. Infants of chronically depressed mothers learn in response to male, but not female, infant-directed speech. *Developmental Psychology* 40 (2): 140–148.

Kashy, D. A., and D. A. Kenny. 2000. The analysis of data from dyads and groups. In *Handbook of research methods in social psychology*, ed. H. T. Reis and C. M. Judd, 451–477. New York: Cambridge University Press.

Kidane, Y., and P. Gloor. 2007. Correlating temporal communication patterns of the Eclipse open source community with performance and creativity. *Computational and Mathematical Organization Theory* 13, no. 1 (March): 17–27.

Kim, T., and A. Pentland. 2007. Enhancing organizational communication using sociometric badges. *Proceedings of the eleventh International Symposium on Wearable Computers*, Boston, October 11–13. See <http://hd.media .mit.edu>.

Lachmann, M., S. Szamado, and C. Bergstrom. 2001. Cost and conflict in animal signals and human language. *PNAS* 98, no. 23 (November 6): 13189–13194.

Laibowitz, M., J. Gips, R. Aylward, A. Pentland, and J. Paradiso. 2006. A sensor network for social dynamics. *Proceedings of the Fifth International Conference on Information Processing in Sensor Networks (IPSN 06)*, 483–491, Nashville, TN, April 19–21.

Lazer, D. 2001. The co-evolution of individual and network. *Journal of Mathematical Sociology* 25, no. 1 (January): 69–108.

Littlepage, G. E., G. W. Schmidt, E. W. Whisler, and A. G. Frost. 1995. An input-process-output analysis of influence and performance in problem-solving groups. *Journal of Personality and Social Psychology* 69 (5): 877–889.

Madan, A. 2006. Social signals in hiring decisions. Working paper. See <http://hd.media.mit.edu>.

Madan, A., and A. Pentland. 2006. VibeFones: Socially aware mobile phones. *Proceedings of the tenth International Symposium on Wearable Computing*, Montreaux, Switzerland, October 11–14. See <http://hd.media.mit .edu>.

Mast, M. S. 2002. Dominance as expressed and inferred through speaking time: A meta-analysis. *Human Communication Research* 28 (3): 420–450.

Milgram, S. 1974. *Obedience to authority: An experimental view.* New York: Harper and Row.

Mowday, R. T. 1981. Review of the group problem solving process: Studies of a valance model. *Academy of Management Review* 6 (1): 170–171.

Nass, C., and S. Brave. 2004. *Voice activated: How people are wired for speech and how computers will speak with us.* Cambridge, MA: MIT Press.

O'Donnell, R. D., and F. T. Eggemeier. 1986. Workload assessment methodology. In *Handbook of perception and performance: Cognitive processes and performance,* ed. K. Boff, L. Kaufman, and J. Thomas, 42.1–42.49. New York: Wiley.

Olguin, D., J. Paradiso, and A. Pentland. 2006. Wearable communicator badge: Designing a new platform for revealing organizational dynamics. *Proceedings of the tenth International Symposium on Wearable Computing,* Montreaux, Switzerland, October 11–14. See <http://hd.media.mit.edu>.

Oliver, N., B. Rosario, and A. Pentland. 2000. A Bayesian computer vision system for modeling human interactions. *IEEE PAMI* 22 (8): 831–843.

Pendergast, W. R. 1990. Managing the negotiation agenda. *Negotiation Journal* 6, no. 2 (April): 135–145.

Pentland, A. 2004. Social dynamics: Signals and behavior. *Proceedings of the International Conference on Developmental Learning,* Salk Institute, San Diego, October 20–22. See <http://hd.media.mit.edu>.

Pentland, A. 2005. Socially aware computation and communication. *IEEE Computer* 38 (3): 33–40.

Pentland, A. 2007a. Automatic mapping and modeling of human networks. *Physica A: Statistical Mechanics and Its Applications* 378 (1): 59–67.

Pentland, A. 2007b. The human nervous system has come alive. In *What are you optimistic about?* ed. J. Brockman. New York: Simon and Schuster.

Pentland, A. 2007c. On the collective nature of human intelligence. *Journal of Adaptive Behavior* 15 (2): 189–198.

Pentland, A., T. Choudhury, N. Eagle, and P. Singh. 2005. Human dynamics: Computation for organizations. *Pattern Recognition Letters* 26 (4): 503–511.

Pianesi, F., M. Zancanaro, B. Lepri, and A. Cappelletti A. Forthcoming. Multimodal annotated corpora of consensus decision making meetings. *Journal of Language Resources and Evaluation.*

Picard, R. 1997. *Affective computing.* Cambridge, MA: MIT Press.

Prelec, D. 2004. A Bayesian truth serum for subjective data. *Science* 306, no. 5695 (October 15): 462–466.

Provine, R. 2001. *Laughter: A scientific investigation.* New York: Penguin Books.

Putnam, H. 1975. The meaning of "meaning." In *Philosophical Papers, Vol. 2: Mind, Language, and Reality.* Cambridge: Cambridge University Press.

Reicher, S., S. Haslam, and M. Platow. 2007. The new psychology of leadership. *Scientific American Mind* 4: 22–29.

Rizzolatti, G., and L. Craighero. 2004. The mirror neuron system. *Annual Review of Neuroscience* 27 (July): 169–192.

Rosenberg, A., and J. Hirschberg. 2005. Acoustic/prosodic and lexical correlates of charismatic speech. *Proceedings of Interspeech 2005,* Lisbon. See <http://www.cs.columbia.edu/speech/papers.cgi>.

Rosenthal, R., and D. B. Rubin. 1982. A simple, general purpose display of magnitude of experimental effects. *Journal of Educational Psychology* 74 (2): 166–169.

Roy, D., and A. Pentland. 2002. Learning words from sights and sounds: A computational model. *Cognitive Science* 26 (1): 113–146.

Simon, H. A. 1995. Explaining the ineffable: AI on the topics of intuition, insight, and inspiration. *Proceedings of the Fourteenth International Joint Conference on Artificial Intelligence* 1: 939–948.

Stewart, K. J., and A. H. Harcourt. 1994. Gorilla vocalizations during rest periods: Signals of impending departure. *Behavior* 130 (1–2): 29–40.

Stoltzman, W. 2006. Toward a social signaling framework: Activity and emphasis in speech. Masters thesis, MIT. See <http://hd.media.mit.edu>.

Sung, M., and A. Pentland. 2005. *PokerMetrics: Stress and lie detection.* MIT human dynamics technical report 594. See <http://hd.media.mit .edu>.

Tetlock, P. 2005. *Expert political judgment: How good is it? How can we know?* Princeton, NJ: Princeton University Press.

Thomas, E. A. C., and T. W. Malone. 1979. On the dynamics of two-person interactions. *Psychological Review* 86: 331–360.

Tiedens, L. Z., and A. R. Fragale. 2003. Power moves: Complementarity in dominant and submissive nonverbal behavior. *Journal of Personality and Social Psychology* 84 (3): 558–568.

Tummolini, L., C. Castelfranchi, E. Pacherie, and J. Dokic. 2006. From mirror neurons to joint actions. *Cognition Systems Research* 7: 101–112.

Valbonesi, L., R. Ansari, D. McNeill, F. Quek, S. Duncan, K. E. McCullough, and R. Bryll. 2002. Multimodal signal analysis of prosody and hand motion: Temporal correlation of speech and gesture. *EUSIPCO 2002*, Tolouse, France, September 2–6.

Van Baaren, R. B., R. W. Holland, B. Steenaert, and A. van Knippenberg. 2003. Mimicry for money: Behavioral consequences of imitation. *Journal of Experimental Social Psychology* 39 (4): 393–398.

Verwey, W. B., and H. A. Veltman. 1996. Detecting short periods of elevated workload: A comparison of nine workload assessment techniques. *Journal of Experimental Psychology: Applied* 2 (3): 270–285.

Waber, A., D. Olguin, T. Kim, A. Mohan, K. Ara, and A. Pentland. 2007. Organizational engineering using sociometric badges. *Proceedings of NetSci:*

International Conference on Network Science, New York, May 20–25. See <http://hd.media.mit.edu>.

Webster, E. C. 1982. *The employment interview: A social judgment process.* Ottawa, ON: S.I.P. Publications.

Webster, E. C., and C. W. Anderson. 1964. *Decision-making in the employment interview.* Montreal, QC: Industrial Relations Centre, McGill University.

Wegner, D. 1995. A computer network model of human transactive memory. *Social Cognition* 13 (3): 319–339.

Werner, S., and E. Keller. 1994. Prosodic aspects of speech. In *Fundamentals of speech synthesis and speech recognition: Basic concepts, state of the art, and future challenges,* ed. E. Keller, 23–40. Chichester, UK: John Wiley.

Whiten, A., J. Goodall, W. McGrew, T. Nishida, V. Reynolds, Y. Sugiyama, C. Tutin, R. Wrangham, and C. Boesch. 1999. Cultures in chimpanzees. *Nature* 399: 682–685.

Wilson, D. 2002. *Darwin's cathedral: Evolution, religion, and the nature of society.* Chicago: University of Chicago Press.

Wilson, D., J. Timmel, and R. Miller. 2004. Cognitive cooperation: When the going gets tough, think as a group. *Human Nature* 15 (3): 225–250.

Wright, O. R. 1969. Summary of research on the selection interview since 1964. *Personnel Psychology* 22: 391–413.

Zahavi, A., and A. Zahavi. 1997. *The handicap principle: A missing piece of Darwin's puzzle.* Oxford: Oxford University Press.

INDEX

Active listening
  customer sales, 25–26
  definition, 23, 25
  groups, 50, 51, 54
  poker, 26
  trade shows, 25
Active listening display, 114–115, 119, 130
Activity
  bluffing, 124–125
  brainstorming, 52–53
  conversations, 142
  correlations with, 104
  customer sales, 118
  definition, 4
  example, 13
  interest, 114

job interviews, 131
measurement, 103–104
negotiation, 120–121, 122
neural substrates, 5
persuasiveness, 116–117
poker, 124–125
purpose of, 13–14
social networking, 14, 77
speed dating, 13–14, 132
Actor partner interdependence model, 120–121
Ambady, Nalini, 99, 100
Ancona, Deborah, 74
Apes, decision making, 35, 58–59, 89
Autism, 39

Bailenson, Jeremy, 11
Bales, Robert, 47
Bavelas, Alexander, 75
Bayesian theory, 60, 62, 63, 69
Bayesian truth serum, 64
Betweenness centrality. *See*
  Centrality
Bluffing, 124–125
Boinski, Sue, 58–59
Brainstorming, 52–53
Brown, Daniel, 88
Buchanan, Mark, 92, 147
Business plan pitch, vii–ix, 16, 28,
  115–117, 126

Campbell, Aimee, 58–59
Carrere, Sybil, 100
Centrality, 78–79, 142
Charisma, 39, 117
Choudury, Tanzeem, 102, 141–142
Clarkson, Brian, 102
Communication overload, 81, 83
Connectors, 142–143
Conscious thought, role of,
  146–147
Consistency
  business plan pitch, 16
  customer sales, 17, 118–119
  definition, 4
  emphasis, 14–15
  example, 15–16
  importance, 105
  interest, 114
  job interviews, 131

measurement, 105
negotiation, 16, 120–123
neural substrates, 5–6, 15–16,
  17
persuasiveness, 116–117
poker, 124–125
purpose of, 15–17
speed dating, 132
stress, 125
trading information, 129
variable emphasis, 16–17, 105
Creativity, 76–77, 92
Cross-validation, 108
Curhan, Jared, 11–12, 119–120
Customer sales, 17, 25–26,
  117–119

Decision accuracy, 110
Digital nervous system, 98
Dijksterhuis, Ap, 146
Dunbar, Robin, 70

Eagle, Nathan, 139–140
Effect size, 110
Electronic communication, 80–82,
  95–98
Empathy, 10, 12, 31, 68
Emphasis. *See* Consistency,
  emphasis
Excitatory hypothesis, 103
Experimental design, 119
Exploring
  dating, 24–25
  definition, 23, 24

groups, 50, 51, 54
trade shows, 24
Exploring display, 130, 133

Galileo, 86
Gips, Jon, 128, 138
Gloor, Peter, 76
Gossip, problem of, 62–65, 69,
70, 148
Gottman, John, 100
Griffiths, Thomas, 147
Group decision making
apes, 35, 58–59, 89
bees, 71–73
evolutionary advantage, 70
examples, 46–47, 57, 58–59
gossip, 62–65, 69, 70, 148
idiots, 62–63, 69, 148
ignorance, 72
information discovery, 72–77, 94
information integration, 59, 72–
77, 94
network effects, xiii–xiv, 89–91,
148–149
primitive humans, 57–58, 70, 73
problems, 48–49
social signaling, xiii, 51–53, 55–56,
57–59, 60–61, 62, 71–73, 89–91
Group roles, 48–49, 50–51, 55
Groupthink, 49, 51, 55, 63

Harcourt, Alexander, 58
Hidden Markov model, 137
Hirschberg, Julia, 117

Honest signals
combinations of (social roles), 19,
22–23, 30, 125–126
definition, x–xiii, 2–3, 17–18
networking hardware, 37–38
neural substrates, 18–19
predicting behavior, 28–30, 92–
93, 111, 113
social interaction, 107–108, 113, 133
social networks, 136
types, in animals, 2, 19
types, in humans, 3–6, 18, 103
use in groups, 43, 50–51, 53–54,
83–84, 89
Hooke, Robert, 85–86
Huberman, Bernardo, 63

Idea markets
Bayesian, 60
bees, 72–73
social signaling, 56, 60–62, 68,
69, 72–73, 145
Idiots, problem of, 62–63, 69, 148
Ignorance, problem of, 72
Infant development, 8, 38
Influence
conversations, 142–143
costs of, 8–9
definition, 4
example of, 6–7
infant development, 8
job interviews, 131
measurement, 104
negotiation, 7, 9, 120–121, 122

Influence (cont.)
  neural substrates, 4–5
  presidential debates, 7–8
  purpose of, 7, 9–10
  social networks, 77–79, 138–139,
    140–141
  uses, 104–105
Influence model, 136–137, 142–143
Information discovery, 72–77, 94
Information influence map,
    143–144
Information integration, 59, 72–77,
    94
Initial reaction effect, 52–53,
    60–61
Interaction process analysis, 47
Interest
  social signals, 113–114

Jaffe, Joseph, 104–105
Jerk-o-meter, 31
Job interviews, 99, 130–131

Kahneman, Daniel, 145
Kidane, Yared, 76

Laughter, 6
Leading
  business plan pitch, 28
  definition, 23, 27–28
  groups, 50, 51
  negotiation, 28, 122
Leading display, 117, 122, 126
Linear regression, 109–110

Madan, Anmol, 114, 130–131, 132
Marital research, 100
Meeting mediator, 56
Method acting, 31
Milgram, Stanley, 54
Mimicry
  definition, 4
  empathy, 10, 12
  job interviews, 131
  measurement, 105–106
  negotiation, 11–12, 40, 120–121, 122
  neural substrates, 5
  purpose of, 10
  sales pitch, 11
  two-way effects, 40–41
  uses, 105–106
Mirror neurons, 5, 10, 37–38
Mood contagion, 39, 53–54

Negotiation
  example, 16, 21–22
  honest signals, 9, 10, 11–12, 16, 40,
    126
  negotiometer, 31
  research findings, 7, 10, 104
  salary negotiations, 9, 11–12, 16,
    28, 40, 119–123
  social roles, 28, 122
Negotiometer, 31
Network intelligence
  definition, xi–xii, xiii–xiv, 62, 89–
    91, 148–149
  gossip, problem of, 64–65, 148
  information flow, 64–65, 67, 77–78

organizations, 80, 90–91
research findings, 65–67
social signaling, 68–70, 89–90,
148–149
uses, xi–xii, xiii–xiv, 66–67, 70,
90–91
Network science, ix–xii

Olguin, Daniel, 102
Optical lens, 86
Organizational engineering, 83–84,
91–92

Paradiso, Joe, 128
Persuasiveness, 116–117
Poker
bluffing, 123–125
example, 33–34, 147
social signaling, 26, 33–34, 61,
67–68, 124–125
Polarization, 49, 51, 55, 63
Prelec, Drazen, 64
Presidential debates, 7–8
Primitive humans, decision
making, 57–58, 70, 73
Provine, Robert, 6

Rosenberg, Andrew, 117
Rosenthal, Robert, 99, 100

Sales calls. See Customer sales
Sensible organizations, 83–84, 91–
92, 144
Simon, Herbert, 147

Smart phones, 139–140
Social circuits
definition, xii–xiii, 38
example, 39
group dynamics, xiii, 51–53, 54,
55–56, 68–70, 82–83, 89–90
network intelligence, 148–149
spread of attitudes, 39, 53–54
Social interaction framework
emotions, 106
honest signals, 107–108
linguistics, 107
Social networks
influence model, 136–137, 142–143
membership, 135–136, 139–141,
143–144
social signaling, 138
Social physics, 92–93, 98
Social prostheses, 31
Social roles, 19, 22–23, 30–31, 49,
69, 122–123, 125, 133
Social signaling
customer sales, 118–119
group decision making, xiii, 51–53,
55–56, 57–59, 60–61, 62, 71–73,
89–91
idea markets, 56, 60–62, 68, 69,
72–73, 145
interest, 113–114
job interviews, 130–131
measurement, 111–112
negotiation, 119–123
network intelligence, 68–70,
89–90

Social signaling (cont.)
  poker, 26, 33–34, 61, 124–125
  predicting behavior, xiii, 35–37,
    41–42
  social fabric, 88–89
  social networks, 138–139
  social roles, 19, 22–23, 30–31, 49,
    69, 122–123, 125, 133
  speed dating, 132–133
  teams, 68, 79–80
  two-way communication, 40–43,
    82–83
  types, 103
Social voting, 59
Sociometer
  background, vii–xi, 87–88,
    101–102
  features, 102
  uses, xiv, 31, 49–51, 55, 83–84,
    89–90, 91, 92–94, 111
Speed dating, 1–3, 13–14, 24–25,
  132–133
Stewart, Kelly, 58
Stoltzman, Will, 115–116,
  117–118
Stress, 124, 125
Sung, Mike, 123–124
Survival exercises, 46–47, 50, 56,
  68

Task roles (in groups), 48–49, 50–
  51, 55
Teaming
  definition, 23, 26–27

  groups, 50, 51, 54
  negotiation, 28, 122
Teaming display, 122, 125, 131
Tenenbaum, Joshua, 147
Tetlock, Philip, 145–146
Thin slice of behavior
  instructor ratings, 99
  job interviews, 99
  marital research, 100
  negotiation study, 119–120,
    121
  social signals, 100–101, 111,
    127
Trade shows, 24, 25, 74
Treasure hunt, 65–67
Tversky, Amos, 145

Unconscious decision making,
  146–147, 150
U.N. meetings, 55

Venture finance experts, vii–ix, 54,
  73

Wilson, David, 70

Yee, Nick, 11

Zancanaro, Massimo, 50
Zimbardo, Phil, 54